D0048666

Permanent Vacation

Permanent Vacation

Twenty Writers on Work and Life in Our National Parks

Volume 1: The West

Editors
Kim Wyatt & Erin Bechtol

Bona Fide Books
Tahoe Paradise, CA

"No Turning Back" by Christa Sadler. First published in *Cañon Journal*, vol. 1, no. 1. Copyright © 1995 by Christa Sadler. Reprinted by permission of author.

"The Traces You Leave" by Nicole Sheets. First published in *Bare Root Review*, Fall 2009. Copyright © 2009 by Nicole Sheets. Reprinted by permission of author.

ISBN 978-1-936511-00-6

2011921969

Cover Art and Design: Bruce Rettig
Photography: Brianna Rettig
Interior Design: Erin Bechtol
Printing and Binding: Thomson-Shore, Dexter, MI

Orders, inquiries, and correspondence should be addressed to:
Bona Fide Books
PO Box 550278, South Lake Tahoe, CA 96155
(530) 573-1513
www.bonafidebooks.com

To the stewards of our national parks.

Contents

Preface

When I was eighteen, I moved to Yosemite National Park. I'd gone there once on a camping trip, and like everyone else, found it incredibly beautiful, and moving in a way I couldn't understand.

I went for a summer and stayed for ten years.

Living in a tent with no electricity, heat, or water suited me. It didn't feel like a hardship; it felt like real life. It was in Yosemite that I became an adult. It was where I learned that I was more than my prescribed family role. In Yosemite, I learned the value of rock, water, and stars, of the natural order of things and my place in it. It was also where I learned about community. In a valley seven miles long, or in a high-country tent camp, the people who served your meals, bagged your groceries, or issued your backcountry permits were your neighbors. They were the people who helped dig your car out of a snowy ditch, and who scared the bears away from your porch. There were few secrets, and lasting friendships were forged.

Some say that those in the park are either running from or hiding from something. As with most clichés, there is likely a bit of truth to this. In hindsight, I can see I left a world that felt too fast for me, far from the natural rhythms of the forest and my body. Spending my formative years in the park, I never learned how to wear lipstick, but I knew how to ford a swollen creek.

While my peers back home were getting married and having children, I was climbing peaks and sleeping under star-bright skies. I was also telling tourists where to find the bathroom.

Living in Yosemite made me a better steward, and maybe even a better person. I was always aware that my home was a place that people saved up all year to come to, for a week or just a weekend. Every interaction was an opportunity to share my love of the park. I am one of those people who smiles when I see families lined up in front of El Capitan for a photo. I recognize that feeling of awe, and believe that as long as humans can conjure that emotion in the presence of nature, we might just have a chance.

A decade after my last day of work—it was the winter of '97, and my belongings had washed down the Merced River in a flood—the park remains my touchstone. Not a day goes by that I don't think about it, and also about the people who helped me become who I am today. I still long for that sense of community, and remain a mountain person who values close ties to people and place. I made this book for others like me, for whom the parks remain a reminder of who they are, and of who they want to be.

Kim Wyatt, Publisher
Yosemite National Park, 1984-1997

Permanent Vacation

Twenty Writers on Work and Life in Our National Parks

Volume 1: The West

The Men I Left Behind

Mary Emerick

Because of the National Park Service, I left enough men behind to field half a baseball team.

I left them because they were too fat, too skinny, too young, too old. They weren't tough enough, or were so tough there was no breaking through their thick skins. One blazed with a toxic cocktail of jealousy and fear. Another drifted along in his own world, no place for anyone else.

I left some because I was afraid I was in love with them, and others because I knew I never could be.

At least those were the reasons I gave myself. Those excuses sounded good in the middle of the night as I drove through a nameless part of Texas, radio a low lullaby, window cracked to let in the smell of the pavement. But the real reason I left was because I had to go and they wanted to stay. Their pull was not as strong as the current of the road.

Every winter I convinced myself that this time I would stay put. After all, they were actually nice guys down at the core. I could make a life with any of them. I would get a real job, put on a skirt, drive to work clutching a coffee mug, and drive home again after a day in an office.

I would stay clean. No more bunkhouses at national park enclaves, no more disappearing into the mountains, no more shoving all my belongings into a pickup, heading out into the unknown. I would give this life a chance. I would learn to cook eggplant parmigiana. Instead of talking about what boot oil to use, my conversations would be about Coach purses or what was on TV. Maybe even football; I could take it that far. On weekends, I would go shopping at the mall. I would dye my hair red. Shave my legs more often. Clean up my language. Curling irons, food processors—I would learn the secrets other women seemed to know.

Each season though, the itch would come and not leave. Nothing made it go away. I always wondered what I was missing. What new park waited to be discovered? Should I go west to Great Basin, south to Carlsbad Caverns? The future hummed with delicious possibility.

For a few men, I tried staying on after the season was over. Staying, wintering over, felt lonely. The country pulled back into itself, brooding; the backpackers that swarmed the trails vanished after Labor Day, leaving them quiet and secretive. Snow fell without a sound. It was like a trap door swinging shut. Shops closed for the season; even the grocery store was scaled down to bare bones. I ran into the veterans—the ones with the real, permanent jobs. "What are you still doing here?" they asked. Sometimes it came out as a challenge. Deep down, I thought they wanted us to be gone; they didn't want to share this place anymore. They wanted us off backpacking through Peru or loading butts on a ski hill, where we belonged. In the spring, after they had time to breathe, we were allowed to show up again, our enthusiasm buoying them for another busy season.

Usually the man I was with could see it coming. It was hard to miss. I weeded through my things, taking bulging garbage bags to Goodwill. I spread atlases out on the kitchen table. I greased my hiking boots. I made phone calls to other women like me. "What's it like out there?" I asked. "How high are the rivers running this year? How's the snowpack? How many people are they hiring?"

Hanging up the phone, I hedged my bets. No, I wasn't leaving. Well, maybe. But just for a little while. I would be back after the change of the seasons. No, it's not you. It's me. The most astute saw it right off. There was no way in hell I was coming back.

The men I left behind were locals, tied by birth or desire to the small towns that fringed the national parks. They sometimes picked up jobs at the park, but they would never leave. This was home for them; these wrinkled valleys and meadows full of amber grasses were places they knew in a way I never could. They meant to raise children here, to die here. They made it clear: I was going to have to choose—the Park Service or them.

After college, unsure of what to do with an optimistic English degree, I had become part of a seasonal tribe, migrating south to north, west to east, every six months. It was the nature of Park Service work: laid off in November, picked up again in May. I'd lived in parks in Nevada, California, New Mexico, and a handful of other states. I saw others like me at the windblown rest stops: cheap cars stuffed with boxes up to the ceiling, skis and bikes piled on top. We nodded in passing, acknowledging kindred spirits. Most of them were alone too. We were brothers and sisters traveling the major arteries of America. To each of us, the road was as familiar as a neighborhood. It was a river carrying us to freedom, away from anything that might want to tie us down.

And the road was a quirky place, full of the absurd and the beautiful. There was the boy who chased me down in a stubby car just outside of Rapid City, brandishing a homemade sign: WOULD YOU LIKE TO SEE MY SHAFT? Another drove naked on I-75. In Texas, a man walked, dragging an enormous cross on his back. A house was burning in Ohio, flames shooting into the sky. I still swear I saw Elvis driving an El Camino on a back road in Oregon.

I drove through suburbs and inner cities and long, two-lane roads dotted with farmhouses. As I passed by, I caught glimpses of someone's life: laundry flapping on the line, a family on the porch. It was strange to think of all the people in the world I would never know.

A butter-colored Chevette was my first road-trip car. It broke down in Roswell, New Mexico; in the middle of nowhere, Nevada; and while crossing a five-mile suspension bridge in Michigan. Each time I patched it together and kept going. The heat quit and the "check engine" light came on and stayed on. I fishtailed in rainstorms and planted it in snow banks. I pushed it to high speeds, discovering that if I hit a cattle guard at eighty, the car would go airborne. I turned up the radio to mask the strange noises coming from under the hood.

I learned how to change the oil, rotate the tires, change out the head gaskets, and put in new brake shoes. Once I labored underneath its low-slung belly for hours, replacing the fuel filter. When I later told one of my friends this, he stared in astonishment: "I thought you weren't supposed to be able to do that yourself!" It never occurred to me to take it in, to have someone else work on it. This car was my ticket out.

"I hope you find what you're looking for," one of the park maintenance guys said as I left yet another place. A thousand miles away, in another town, a man in a bar said almost the same thing. "A lot of people come here looking for something. But if you don't bring it with you, you won't find it here." I just shook my head. Stuck in one place, what did they know?

I tried to learn how to whistle as I drove. I learned that if you chewed too much cinnamon gum, you could burn your tongue. I coached myself through dangerous situations: tornados in Amarillo, merging traffic in Atlanta. I could tell what part of the country I was in by the radio stations. There were the more sedate Ws that heralded my return across the Mississippi, and the brash Ks of the West. Sometimes the only station I could tune in to carried the anguished voice of a radio host, railing against injustice. I drove in and out of the reach of the stations, music fading and reappearing. I was in a cocoon, rocketing along, untouchable.

These drives had a sense of nameless urgency to them. I sometimes drove deep into the night, featureless buildings passing by in a blur. There was always the hope of making it farther. I redlined the gas gauge, grudging the time it would take to fill up. In the long stretches of Utah and Nevada, I coasted in on fumes more than once.

I saw car crashes, overturned semis, flashing lights signaling tragedy belonging to someone else. But most of the time there was sameness, a security to these road trips. I liked turning another page in the road map, the odometer steadily clicking away the miles.

The men I left behind reacted in different ways. Some cut all ties immediately. Others tried to hang on with desperate phone calls from several states away. "I won't wait forever," they warned. And most didn't, marrying stay-at-home girls. Some did wait though, for years, their letters gradually winding down to the occasional, insincere Christmas card and then tapering off. A few I lost track of, like footprints in snow.

I felt a mixture of relief and pain. Sometimes I wanted them to run after me, throwing a backpack in the car. Another part of me couldn't get out of there fast enough. It was always a test they could never pass. If there were tears, they were long gone by the time I merged onto the interstate. Instead, the destination became my new crush. I dreamed of its contours as I slept beneath clammy nylon in roadside campgrounds, or behind flimsy curtains of truck-stop motels. That familiar brown Park Service sign made my heart beat faster. This would be the one, the place that I would never leave.

"I have a problem with commitment," I said for years to justify my never staying put with one person or with one place. I said it, but it wasn't really true. I had no problem falling in love with the sharp edges of a mountain range, or with a sweet pair of blue eyes. It was only a few months down the road that I realized what choosing to stay would mean. There would be no more long, barefoot drives, hair wild and loose, forearm turning brown out the left-hand window. No more sweating water bottle clamped between my thighs, no more gradual change of the country as I drove. No more waking up wondering which state I was in. There would be no more anticipation, no more possibility, nothing that could make my heart beat faster with the scary unknown. The landscape I looked at now would be the same one from now to eternity.

There were some men whose memories stayed with me. Their faces ran through my mind as I lay in my sleeping bag. There was the one who lived in a teepee close to the water's edge, whose handlebars I rode as we swept through the heart of our small island. There was the one who taught me to fly-fish knee -deep in the Yellowstone River. Thinking of them, regret crept in like smoke.

But at the parks, we spoke a common language. We wore the same clothes: pilled, old Patagonia fleece, Teva sandals. We all needed haircuts. At the first potlucks of the season, in the bunkhouses, we started the same ritual.

"You worked at Big Cypress? Did you know Mike Patten?"

"The General! Sure did. Just stopped by to see him in Missoula."

"What year were you at Sequoia? No way, I was there then too; I lived at Grant Grove. Did you ever make it up to Granite Basin?"

"Killer hike! Say, were you on the Yellowstone fires?"

"Wasn't everyone?"

You could spend hours at this game. These people were my new adopted family. They understood why I labored to identify a small, feathery fern or slogged up a talus slope just to watch the sun set. They understood the nearly mythical turning of the atlas page, the sweet green sweep of a park seen for the first time from a scenic overlook. The men I left behind could never compete.

I have lived on an island in Alaska for almost seven years now— longer than I have lived anywhere in my adult life. I have let myself sink into the country instead of skirting its boundaries. Staying put, I've noticed what I never did in all the years of moving on. The view might look the same, but there are subtle differences you pick up when you grow familiar with the same mountain's shoulder, the same expanse of sea. There is fresh snow on the peaks that wasn't there yesterday. The tide is lower, exposing the abalones on the rock shelf. You can say that this is the coldest, or the wettest, or the hottest summer you can remember in all the summers you have lived here without sounding foolish.

I miss the seasonal life sometimes. It was simple, uncomplicated, not like staying is. Staying means you face up to yourself in the mirror instead of running away. If you don't like a job or want out of a bad situation, you can't just hop in the car and leave it all behind. You have to let someone you love slip through the cracks in your armor.

My ancient road atlas sits on the desk by my computer. It is the only thing that has stayed with me in all the years of travel. Sometimes I can't resist the urge to riffle through the crumpled maps. Each page is a memory of my younger self, all the highways that have led me to this place.

I've joined the ranks of the veterans, those who stay year -round. I gave up the seasonal Park Service life years ago for a deskbound Forest Service one. It seemed like the right choice—I didn't want to leave anyone behind anymore. I fell in love. I got married. My friends, still gutting it out in the seasonal trenches, laughed, unbelieving.

"The last of the great ones falls," they said. "When are you coming back down south?"

The seasonals who leave in the fall don't live here through the torrential rainstorms that can last the entire month of November. They don't have to shovel. They don't lose minutes of daylight each day, all the light in the sky slowly being squeezed down to a few precious hours. In turn, though, they don't really know this moody island.

Sometimes I almost dread the seasonals' return. They blow in from all corners of the globe, with tales of skiing in Antarctica, mountain climbing in Nepal. "I used to be like you," I want to say, but I don't know if they would believe it. "I couldn't ever have a desk job," one earnestly tells me.

Hold out, I want to tell them. Fight it for as long as you can. People will tell you that you need a permanent job, a ladder, a lawnmower, a mortgage. "How come you're still single?" they will ask, with equal parts distrust and pity. Don't listen. Pack up your stuff, say goodbye, and drive on, sister. The road is waiting.

A Portrait of My Father in Three Places

Cassandra Kircher

Wyoming, 1965

I'm ten the first time my father takes us camping in a national park. Yellowstone, except we're staying next door at Jenny Lake Campground in Teton National Park, because my dad likes it better. "Fewer people," he says, even though this campground is full too. My dad has already learned the ropes around here—how to get a campsite, where to buy ice for the cooler he keeps right outside the tent door—and I like Jenny Lake. Not that I don't like camping in other places, like South Dakota, where we've been before. But this feels like real camping to me. I like how we see herds of wild deer, and how it gets so cold at night we have to put on our winter coats just to sit around the campfire.

When it's time for bed that first night, we sleep on air mattresses in flannel sleeping bags. One of my brothers sleeps beside me, and my littlest brother sleeps beside him. I can hear my father sprinkling water on our fire—the hot coals hissing when the water hits them, the smell of smoke all the way in the tent—and then moving around, making our camp safe. I hear him lock the car. When he comes into our home, he unzips the heavy door and stretches out beside my mom like a guard.

Nothing outside the tent is moving, not even the breeze. I picture the moon somewhere up high.

"Goodnight," my dad says into the perfect square of the tent, and everyone says goodnight right back.

This is when our story happens. Not right then, but an hour or two later, when we all wake up to snoring, and no one says a thing. No one moves, not even my littlest brother. Instead, we lie stiff and tense like logs, listening to a snoring that can't be my father but must be something.

"Grizzly," my mom whispers. My stomach flips, and my father gets ready to protect his family like he's supposed to.

"Don't move," he says, and from there, everything happens fast. My father slips out of his sleeping bag and stands. He steps in the dark to the door. In his right hand he is holding something; in his left hand he is holding something else.

My father says nothing. The bear growls from right outside. A sound like slobber. I close my eyes. I hear the tent unzip, and I open them. When I look to the door, I see my father facing the bear. He raises one hand and turns on his flashlight; he raises his other hand and sprays out the bug spray called Off. Everything is aimed right toward the bear.

The next morning my body feels the lines on the air mattress, and I smell earth and canvas. The sun is gold and awake. Outside I hear the campfire burp and snap, the low voices of my father and mother, and the hollowness of heavy boots on dry, packed dirt as my father checks on something by the picnic table. The air is cold. My brothers' heads are lost in their sleeping bags, and I slip on my jacket and race for my favorite cereal—the kind that comes in little boxes, that we all three like and fight over and get only for vacations.

When I come out of the tent, breakfast isn't ready, and even from a distance I can tell our aqua cooler has been through something bad. Its lock is all bent up, and instead of being beside the tent door where I saw it last, it's sitting on the picnic table surrounded by all the food that used to be inside its cold belly: the cheese, eggs, and butter. A carton of milk. They all look different.

"Compliments of our visitor," my father says, and for a moment I imagine our visitor as a furless and weak park ranger coming by after I was asleep.

It takes everything I have to remain calm as I remember what happened—that just a few hours ago, in the black of the night, my father was a hero, saving our lives as he greeted the grizzly.

Montana, 1972

I'm seventeen. My dad, my mom, my brothers, and I are on vacation, driving across Nebraska and Wyoming in our Ford LTD before making a right-hand turn at Colter Bay and heading up to Glacier National Park. Behind the Ford we're pulling a wooden pop-up camper, one that is hand-built and swerves in the wake of our exhaust like a water-skier. My father has picked it up from the want ads.

My father has picked up a lot of new equipment for this trip: five down sleeping bags, five foam air mattresses, five rectangular backpacks, and a whole fleet of plastic containers recommended—according to my father—by camping experts: a tube for peanut butter, another for mayonnaise, a carton molded to nest half a dozen medium-sized eggs. He buys everything one afternoon from The Back Woods, the only mountaineering store in Omaha. He also purchases an expedition tent, in which my youngest brother and I will sleep. The tent features a snow tunnel and a little half-moon panel that can be zipped out of the floor in case you want to light a stove indoors and brew a cup of tea during a blizzard.

"I think," my brother says with a maturity way beyond his twelve years, "that Dad might be feeling his midlife."

I'm not sure about anyone else, but my father seems to be thinking of this vacation as our family's manifest destiny, our great northern adventure and a step above the Teton National Park area, where we have camped for several years. At a gas station south of Flathead Lake, he picks up a copy of *Night of the Grizzlies* for us to share during our next two weeks of relaxation. He'd heard of the book back in Omaha, and even though he knows it focuses on two bears that maul two different park visitors in two different areas of Glacier National Park on the same night, he buys it, because he somehow thinks it will help familiarize us with Glacier's topography and emergency procedures—not to mention the park's flora and, especially, its fauna.

After we arrive, the three of us kids register complaints, as if that's our job: "The tent is too small," we say. "The air is too cold." "The sky is too dark." My parents don't respond—just get quiet in a way that's typical. The bottom line is, we really don't have much to complain about. It's true that our fluffy sleeping bags aren't rated for Glacier National Park temperatures. It's also true that the trout just aren't biting. But a bigger truth is probably that we kids are suffering from a case of growing older, which keeps us from enjoying a camping trip like this one this particular year. In the past, fly-fishing was our No. 1 activity, and all three of us were always ready to go out and cast by our father's side like shadows. This year he's lucky to have one of us following along. My youngest brother, in what I guess is a show of solidarity with his teenage siblings, even refuses to wear his waders.

Most mornings my father fishes alone, coming back for lunch empty-handed and frustrated. Most afternoons we hike Glacier's trails. By day two, when we surprise a grizzly eating huckleberries beside Hidden Lake, all five of us have read through Chapter Four of *Night of the Grizzlies,* and my father finally decides to purchase the bells we have seen other hikers wearing. These little backpacking gems warn bears that you are present, sort of like a doorbell. But instead of being frugal, my father overbuys and ties several bells onto each of our fanny packs so that we look and sound like reindeer, or a small, moving cathedral.

After dinner most evenings, we walk over to the amphitheatre and listen to the free campfire programs offered by the Park Service. It's my father who makes us attend these productions. I'm not sure about my brothers, but I resent sitting on a log looking at slides of the tundra when most kids my age are attending rock concerts somewhere. On our fourth night at the amphitheatre, I know we're in trouble with a program called something as boring as "Trout Fishing in Glacier National Park." The ranger in charge—a real go-getter—talks about how he's been fishing a place called Goat Lake on his days off. It's hard hiking to get there, he says, but worth every uphill step. He even recommends using a fly called, for God's sake, the Yellow Humpy, and he shows us a couple slides of other flies he has wasted valuable time tying. Not two minutes into the program, I notice my father taking notes in the margins of our park map.

When we return to the campsite, my father radiates enthusiasm. "Goat Lake, anyone?" he asks in a happy voice, spreading the map out on the picnic table. In the glow of our Coleman lantern, I follow his index finger over masses of topographical lines up to a tiny blue oval.

"Dad," I say, after a few minutes of studying the situation, "Goat Lake is eight miles into the backcountry—it's in Canada."

"It's nothing but a personal theory," my father says, "but I think fishing another country's waters will bring us luck."

In the morning my father's voice has changed from animated to mute—a pattern so familiar to me that I think all fathers stop talking when they are upset or angry, and that all daughters spend energy worrying about them and trying to get them to smile. As he silently herds us into the car, I realize that my father might be something more serious than "a pill," the term my mother sometimes uses in reference to him. He might, in fact, be a difficult man—a hunch that I've been considering for a couple years now, and one that rings true once we arrive at the Goat Lake trailhead and he retrieves his pole, creel, and backpack from the trunk of the LTD with such speed and purpose that I feel as if I'm watching a cartoon in fast-forward.

None of us expects what happens next: My father doesn't even say goodbye to his loving family. Instead he puts himself in high gear and storms up the trail as quickly as a six-foot-three man can storm.

"Dad," I say in a loud-enough voice. "Your bear bells . . ."

Not one of us follows. Instead we assess our own situation. The chance of our father returning to the car soon is not good, but it is possible. If we leave to go horseback riding or to drive the Going to the Sun Highway, or even to hang out in the Many Glacier Hotel lobby, my father will have a problem: there is no phone close by. There is not much of anything, really, and only a couple other cars—dusty ones that look as if they have been there for days—sit at the trailhead. I don't get the feeling that this place is a hip tourist destination.

My mother is in a bind. At least that must be what she is thinking, now that she is in charge. It's not as if she can sit the three of us down and start up a discussion about her husband's behavior. In the unspoken way that our family oftentimes communicates, however, we all seem to agree that the best option is to wait for our father right where we are. So that's what we do.

At one point, both my brothers get out their fishing poles and start to cast into a nearby pond. At another point, my mother stretches out on the backseat and naps. There is not a lot of talking. There is no complaining. The sun shines, and there is that quiet that I look for in nature. After lunch, I take a little hike around the area and admire a field of just-blooming bluebells. When I return, I stop to watch my brothers release a ten- to twelve-inch brook trout back into the clear water.

At sunset my father finally comes down the trail, and I can tell, even from a distance, that his mood hasn't changed. We all watch him stash his fishing gear into the trunk, take his car keys out of the pocket of his fishing shorts, and get behind the steering wheel.

"Let's go," he says, and at first I think he means back to the campground. When we arrive at our site and he begins taking down the backpacking tent and folding up our pop-up camper, I realize that those words mean something else, and that we will miss tonight's campfire program and leave this national park for good.

The next hour, we break camp so fast I feel dizzy.

An hour later, when we are driving past Flathead Lake with our pop-up camper, I start thinking about motels. It is ink black out, and not much traffic is on the two-lane highway. At the next gas station, my mom decides to sit in the back—to be honest, I think she is getting tired of sitting so close to all that silence—and I end up being the one moving up beside my dad. I don't ask to drive.

"Dad," I say after another hundred miles, "where are we going?"

"Jenny Lake," he says, surprising me by saying anything at all. "That campground in the Tetons."

"We're camping tonight?" I say.

"Not tonight. It'll be full. We'll be there about dawn, the first car in line for tomorrow."

"We're not sleeping?" I ask, impressed at how well my father has thought everything through.

"Go ahead and sleep," he says.

North of Yellowstone I am still awake. In the backseat, my mother and brothers are not. A wind has come up, and the car careens back and forth in the lane. We're probably going too fast, if rules like that even apply out here on these back roads. My father hasn't talked again for miles. He just stares straight ahead into the blackness, and I'm doing the same.

That's when the buck appears in our headlights. Tall and beautiful, his neck turned with so much grace that he looks like a dancer. His eyes big, shiny globes looking straight at us. In that moment, I think he must be an apparition. But then the LTD crashes into his huge body. The animal crumbles, folds forward over himself, his head and antlers bowing toward us. And there is sound—the hollow sound of metal hitting flesh, hitting something alive—and everyone in the car is awake.

"John!" my mother says.

My father and I get out of the car, we all get out of the car, and look at the huge dent in the hood. There is damage, and there are little brown hairs stuck in the fender at the place where the paint has been disturbed. There is no buck lying in front of the car—just the space of where he has been, the space of impact. The car's engine is still running.

"Maybe he's okay," I say, but I know—we all are old enough to know—that he isn't, that just beyond the headlights, he is in the biggest trouble ever. I want to suggest that we help him, but

I know that we can't, and that to say such a thing out loud would be ridiculous from someone my age. At one point, either my father or mother says the word "insurance."

When we get back in the car, my mother takes my place in the front seat, and everything else is different too. I'm guessing that everything will stay different, all the way through Yellowstone National Park to its smaller cousin, the Tetons, where we will probably be the first in line at Jenny Lake Campground, just as my father predicts. A mangled car waiting for the ranger to come on duty so we can claim a vacant space, the sun just pushing up into the sky. Until then we'll drive with nothing but black out the window, my father's hand gripping the steering wheel, tightly trying to keep control.

Colorado, 1982

I'm twenty-seven when my father drives alone across Nebraska to visit me in Rocky Mountain National Park because he's retired now and my mother is not, and neither of my brothers lives at home. My father has bought brand-new hiking clothes for the trip: shorts with pockets, big boots, a lightweight button-down shirt that looks stiff. For the past six years, I have worked in the park as a ranger, and my father has coordinated this visit with my tour of duty at the Lawn Lake Patrol Cabin, 5.2 miles into the backcountry. He has packed in his fly rod, and on the way up the trail, I see him eyeing Roaring River for trout. Later, at just the right spot in the clearing, I turn him around so he can see faraway Longs Peak framed, like a surprise, by the aspen, but he doesn't seem interested in dry landscape.

When we arrive at the cabin, my father watches me unbolt the three windows and unlock the padlock on the heavy door as if he can't believe his daughter can do these kinds of things. I don't get the feeling that he thinks me incompetent as much as I sense that these workaday duties aren't part of his master plan. Once we're inside, there are other chores: unpacking the food, airing the bedding, building the fire. My father agrees to get water from the lake, but when I hand him the ten-gallon collapsible plastic jug, I find myself worrying that even the empty receptacle is too heavy for him. During dinner, my Park Service–issue radio is on, but it's mostly static, the way it always is when I'm in this drainage. It makes the discomfort I'm feeling audible.

"See any trout at the lake?" I say, wondering what other daughters would mention to their sullen father in a twelve-by-twelve-foot backcountry cabin.

"Not really," he says, and I push another log into the stove. Early the next morning, my father carries his fishing gear out the door slowly, as if his heart hurts, and I go down to the lake with him. The water is slick and clear, not like a mirror as much as a window I can't see through to the bottom. In spite of his interest in trout fishing, my father is a north-woods-lake man, and he doesn't seem to admire this high-altitude water. Instead he works at tying on a fly, some kind of streamer—probably one he's been deciding on since we arrived.

I love the cork handle of his fishing pole, the way my father's hand wraps around it as he begins to fish—stopping and starting at first, like an engine trying to get going, and then really beginning to cast, the pole an extension of his long arm as he stretches an arc over the water. For the longest time, I stand there feeling the rhythm of the casting, remembering how I used to mimic him with my own pole, back and forth, admiring the grace of his movements, the concentration in every muscle. What I think about most, as I leave him for a short patrol of the four Lawn Lake campsites, is my father's intention: to manipulate a fly so that it skits and lights in a way that looks like an insect, and not like the simulation that it is. When I return he has caught one cutthroat, which he's placed in the dark-green backpacking creel he's brought along on this trip. I can't tell if he's pleased with his catch or not.

Back when we used to camp as a family, and my father caught all the fish he was allowed to catch on a single day, he would clean them and put them on ice in our cooler. I only saw him perform the cleaning ritual once—saw him make a short, sharp cut across the fish's throat with his knife before slicing its underbelly in one long line from tail to jaw. This was when I felt sick, when I saw my father, without a second thought, hold a fish by its mouth with one hand and pull its insides out with his other so that they were visible for anyone to see.

"This is the bloodline," my father said next, as he put his hand in the fish's belly again and scraped away a brown-and-red streak. "All of it comes out." He left the head on. As far as I know, my father never beheaded a trout—maybe out of respect, maybe because acknowledging a meal's origins seems most honest to him.

Although I never saw my father clean fish again, I usually watched him prepare them—watched him roll the fish in flour, salt and pepper them on both sides, and put them in the metal lid of the huge family mess kit that served as our frying pan in the wild. When I was a kid, I didn't eat trout, but I liked smelling them cook, and I liked their brown-gold color against the silver of the pan. My father sautéed them in butter, and even though they looked like works of art when he finished, I don't think my mother liked making them part of her meal. Now I eat trout— not that I fish for them or buy them to prepare myself, not that I forget about how svelte and flashing they look in the wild. But each summer, when my parents visit me in Estes Park, we eat at the Sundeck Restaurant, and my mother orders French toast for breakfast, while my father and I order Rocky Mountain trout, served stiff and whole across our plates.

When my father catches his cutthroat at the Lawn Lake cabin, I expect him to clean it like he used to when I was a child, and I am surprised when he instead goes into the cabin and comes out with the biggest cooking pot he can find before taking it down to the lake and filling it. After that, he transfers the trout from his creel to the silver pot, where it barely has room to swim, and carries it up to the cement stoop of the cabin, where he leaves it all afternoon. At dusk I watch my father bring his trout inside with us for the night, like a pet, and I wonder if he plans to feed it.

On our second day out, I'm scheduled to patrol up to Rowe Glacier, and my father chooses to stay behind at the lake and fish. Because it's a strenuous hike, I don't try hard to persuade him to come along, but I regret that he'll miss being in a place where the view extends out beyond the tundra to the clouds. As my father prepares his line, tying on a new fly on a new leader, I adjust my daypack before putting my radio in its holster and starting off. It's a day of sun and cloudless skies. Little pink and purple pincushions grow close to the ground—the only way they can at 11,000 feet—and with each step, I feel the tension from the cabin dissolve.

When I reach Mummy Pass, I look down and see my father at the east edge of the lake, his arm casting back and forth, as if he is waving to me. Except the wave is strange and weak, and it makes me a little sad to watch him, and I turn away and keep hiking.

On my way back down, several hours later, I patrol through the four campsites, but no one is there for the night, and I have the sense that my father and I are the only people in this landscape. Back at the cabin, I find him sitting on the cement stoop. The air around him smells like pine. Beside him is the cook pot, and when I look down into it, there is not one, but two trout corralled together, side-by-side and swimming in place, each eyeing the other from the side of its head.

"Dinner?" I ask, gesturing toward the pot, wondering if my father was waiting all along to catch two trout before he cleaned one.

Finally, he speaks. "I can't kill them," he says, and for a moment I feel a flash of fear, that kind of fear I've felt all my life whenever my father seems vulnerable. Instead of responding, I unzip a side pocket of my pack, get out my water bottle, offer my father a drink, and take a long one myself, thinking it would be easier to be back up at the glacier, eating my lunch alone on a flat rock.

"What are you doing with these fish?" I ask, wondering if he wants me to clean them, wondering if he wants to release them, wondering if they are, perhaps, even too small to keep. My father says nothing. "I thought you liked trout," I say.

Instead of responding, he picks up the cook pot and brings it inside. I watch my father light the Coleman lantern and the Coleman stove—just like he used to light them when I was a kid. We have spaghetti and tomato sauce for dinner, and I notice that, in spite of his fishing luck, my father has little energy. For the rest of the evening, he reminds me of a statue, his face chiseled with lines, his brown eyes less bright than ever before.

When I wake on the third day, my father is sitting in a chair by the wood box, looking all wrong without a newspaper on his lap. There's rain—I can hear it and smell it, and my father is watching it out the window, thinking about something far away from this cabin. It's hard for me to see him, wherever he's at in the past. I'd rather have him here in the present, talking with the charm and humor he's capable of, or fishing down at the lake, holding the extra loop of line with his left hand, hearing the *click, click, click* as he slowly winds his reel, trolling his fly on top of the water.

"Are you okay, Dad?" I ask. He hasn't shaved since we've been here, and he looks changed.

My father doesn't even try to tell me how he feels. Instead he asks me what is on my agenda for the day, and I think about all I should be doing to post the sign way down at Upper Tileston Meadows: the deep hole I should be digging, the tree I should be felling, the soil I should be tamping down so that the park's message to campers stays up straight and strong.

"With this rain, it's hard to say," I answer, thinking that I should probably stay put in the cabin and sharpen the axes or shovels instead of trying to keep up with the outdoor chores. And there's always the food in the cabinet to sort through.

On the floor, my father arranges pieces of bark with his foot like he's playing a game, creating a whole world that is more real to him than the one he is in. I have no idea if he is acting this way because he's unhappy with the way I'm living my life, or because he's unhappy with the way he's lived his. I have no idea if he feels the shift in our relationship, or if all of his sadness is the sign of something larger. As I look over at him, I realize that I don't know what it feels like to be older and feebler than you'd like to be. What I do know is that I miss him—his way of knowing and seeing the world, his way of making me feel safe, like when I was a kid. And I know that I'm aware of the arc of a life that is his.

But I don't mention any of what I'm struggling with. Instead I open up the faded ranger logbook, sit down at the table, and begin catching up on the entries that are part of my job.

Later, when the rain lets up a little, my father goes out on the stoop, carrying his aluminum fly box, and I wonder about the two trout in the bucket in the corner—a scene I'd come to think of as "Still Life with Fish." I wonder about all the sun that they're not getting in this cavelike cabin, and about all the air filled with smoke and carbon dioxide from the old wood-burning stove. Finally, I have the nerve to walk over to the corner and look down into the metal cook pot. At first I can only see blackness and shadows, swirling like a kaleidoscope, and then I begin to make out the two trout suspended in water. When I see them and understand what they are, I know, in a moment, that they are dying. Their backs have the white film of death on them. And they are lilting sideways, their whole bodies caving in to the pull they are feeling.

Nine Ways of Looking at a Giant Sequoia

Monica Delmartini

First Look

I'm seven years old, in tiny boots, and my parents are showing me the world's largest tree. I'm impressed, of course, by the tree's size—the way its orangey gleams jump out of the woods—but it's a little hard to connect with, what with the fence and the sign, the milling visitors, the arbitrary association with a long-dead Civil War general. I notice the tree, but I notice the rest of the forest too—the foreign, piney taste of the air, the towering canopy, the singing birds.

What really grabs me, later that day, is the river. I crouch on the wet sand and stare and stare into the water, perfectly clear blue–green pooling over peppered cobbles, flecks of mica swirling like glitter. All of it strange and new and exactly right, the most perfect water I've ever seen. Trout hang in the current like dark submarines, and the current pours foamy white between the boulders and spreads out across the middle of the pool. And the crisp edges fan out across the fish, and the breathing green depths become a scalloped parade of lacy small backward-curling wavelets, all shining and champagne in the low afternoon light. And the river goes jumping—down across the rounded backs of the boulders and caught up and sprayed in flecks of dampness and leaping mists and all of it backlit like a thousand sparklers.

And I never get over it.

Burning (1)

The Sierra in August: hot Jeffrey pine cream-soda smell, pine dust, sticky pitch, pennyroyal sweetness, pockets of damp-green smell in ferny places, mineral in the air, dark sparkledust. And wraithed around the landscape, the thrill of char—serious, acrid, and sweet, lightning strike, burst sapwood, smolder for days and then jump out and spread.

Standing on Silliman Pass three days after a storm, I could count them: strike, strike, strike, strike; tiny smoke plumes, single trees. A week, two weeks, three weeks later, and they've moved and merged and the smoke blows in fat columns. Silliman Pass: broad and sandy, 10,000 feet, bare creamy granite and scattered Western white pine, high, airy place with the sound of the moving air and the silence and the starshine ringing across a sixty-mile view of open space and upthrust peaks. Nightfall and wind shift and the smoke settles on me in my sleeping bag, pitch dripping, late summer, the smoke smell waking me through the night in primal animal alert.

Giant Forest burning at night: all through the day the forest is choke-smoky and the visitors complain. At night, no one on the road, everyone tucked away in a campground, toasting marshmallows and playing hearts by Coleman lantern. No one out, the whole park empty, one could take a nap in the middle of the road. Giant Forest burning and the woods luminous with the fire that's too small and smoky to see by day. Lines and wreathes, tiny tongues, silhouettes of giants with fire gnawing the edges of old scars, soft orange glow everywhere, and then—up at the head of a narrow draw, perfectly framed and only visible for a moment, one tree roaring in white–orange flames like a god come to life in its niche.

In the morning the smoke pools near the ground, and I drive slowly between visitor centers, watching a firefighter poke the forest edge with a shovel. She has long, blonde braids. She. A girl, like me, playing with fire. My freshly laundered uniform is suddenly completely unacceptable.

Winter

It's been five days since the last storm, giving the trees a chance to shake the snow out of their branches, the squirrels to print the buried road with their little hops. We practice our hops too, laughing and postholing and climbing over logs, wiping our wet and lichen-crumbed hands on our jeans. It's too warm for jackets, but icicles hang from shady cracks in the famous old sequoia logs.

We find the meadow frozen solid, slick as a skating rink and dusted in drifts. I slide one boot after the other out to the channel, jump up and down experimentally. Not even a creak. I've never felt the forest so empty—just ourselves, one nuthatch singing, and a patch of bloodied snow where a squirrel no longer was. Coyote tracks. I know there are bears stuffed into hollow logs, frogs dug down someplace where they aren't frozen through, bracken ferns waiting under the snow with their shoots in balled fists, pine martens doing whatever it is they do in the winter. But our only company is the sound of the air sighing and sighing in the trees, and the snow angels we make in the middle of the meadow. Until we meet the only other human abroad in Giant Forest, stumping along in earmuffs and snowshoes. We make small talk, he asks where we're from, and I say "Here," and grin. I don't even try to sound humble. "This is my office."

On our way back, we keep an eye out for our tree—somehow,

it's become "our" tree, just like a grove of ancient trees has become "my" office. And we find it, improbably still upright, a gnawed-on black hulk standing up in the sky, where it might still be standing in five hundred years.

Burning (2)

A long morning of huddling in our sweatshirts and stamping our boots, standing in circles to chat, taping maps to the sides of trucks, blowing on our fingers. But finally we're strung out along the roadway and something is happening just around the corner. I've been looking forward to this for, well, years, but when I catch my first whiff of smoke, I suddenly have to squash the urge to leave, and quickly. The smoke thickens, it rolls my way, it alters the light. And, standing in a patch of copper sun in a too-clean shirt two sizes too big for me, I find myself leaning away, unreasonably alarmed. In fire school we lit off big swaths of grassy hillside and then chased after the flames with hoses, but this feels different. Big. Serious. And then comes the firing team around the corner, all of them smiling as they drag little lines of flame behind them, and the alarm fades, and now I'm leaning in, toward the fire, rapt as the flames stay small, as they nose around in the duff, bump into the foamy bark of the tree in front of me, gutter a while, and go out.

Time passes, and the day starts to make more sense. I get less clean. The smoke lies down, roiling and brown across the road, and we cough and squint. I'm on a squad made up almost entirely of women, and we patrol our section of road, smiling at each other, squinting, finding nothing out of the ordinary until a towering dead sequoia, blackened from toe to broken head by past fires, catches alight and starts to burn in earnest, doing its best impression of the fireworks we used to take to the safe, inflammable beach when I was a kid: WARNING: EMITS SHOWER OF SPARKS. DO NOT HOLD IN HAND. LIGHT FUSE AND GET AWAY.

The old trunk pops and cracks and geysers burning embers across the line, and we dash around like squirrels, swatting out tiny fires. We keep this up until the sun starts to set and the wind shifts, carrying the smoke and glowing debris downhill, away from us, and we sit down on a log to rest, thirteen hours into our workday, and I notice my feet howling at me. We dig out snacks and headlamps and the forest darkens around us, the glow of hundreds of smoldering bits of wood finally emerging from the smoke. I could watch the fire slowly chew into the logs all night, but it's time for our squad to leave, so we turn and hike down the road, away from the still-burning tree, and the moment we're around the corner, the entire forest lights up in a pink explosion: the old tree finally let a huge piece of itself drop. I hear the simultaneous voices of two dozen firefighters, still tucked away in the dark woods, sighing, "Ooooh . . . "

Spring

The meadow looks like it just got out of bed. Last year's vegetation is squashed flat and brown, chunks of snow lie here and there, the water is still figuring out how to flow across it. The corn lilies have just started to sprout, pushing up through the lank dead stuff in great, rounded points. The forest floor looks matted and damp, orange slime mold starts to stipple the ash, and the trees are up to something, no doubt, in their trunks, but look imperturbable as ever. All the action is on the ground, along the trail edges and in seepy places where the bracken and the big meadow plants are nudging upward. And audible from half a mile away, an utter cacophony: every Pacific tree frog in the forest yelling at the top of its little lungs, and the sound is unwavering, solid. There could be birds singing, but who could hear them?

Springtime unspools quickly in the mountains—a brief,

green frenzy between the calm hush of winter and the calm thrum of summer. The meadow turns hot green, and bears come out to eat the new plants, grazing like cows in the clearings.

Summer

"There's only one way to look at a giant sequoia," one of my colleagues announces during an orientation hike at the beginning of my first summer working in the park. "Lying on your back at the foot of it, looking straight up." We all try it. He's right.

Glory season. Wildflower season. Backpacking season. Skinny-dipping season. Season of sweet-scented dark sparkle-dust and pine duff, of idle fishing, of laughing woodpeckers, of the curving sky and the embarrassment of stars above my sleeping bag. Tourist season, if you must. Fire season. Before Giant Forest became my office, it was my living room, my lounge, my photography studio, my writing desk, my napping spot. Mornings would find me on my knees in the meadow, my macro lens stuck down the throat of a dewy camas flower. Afternoons I'd pad deep into the forest in moccasins with a thermos of gin and tonic. Summertime, and the woods are humming and lively. Bear cubs frolic like monkeys in the trees. Great washes of lupine appear on the forest floor and hang their candy smell all over the air. Garter snakes stalk frogs in the meadow, and the meadow parades through its shifting palette— lilac and purple, then orange and yellow, then red and white, then just white, waving above the grass as it begins to burnish. Hundreds of birds singing, hundreds of squirrels chasing each other in dizzy spirals. Ten thousand new tree seedlings poking their heads out of last year's ash. The big trees stand there, looking imperturbable, but their pollen sifts down onto everything below. We startle bears in pairs out of the lupine.

I have a favorite sequoia, of course, and a favorite spot in which to lie and admire it. It's typically massive, typically copper-barked, typically disorienting and unlikely looking, no doubt incredibly old but still vigorous and lushly crowned. And it's had fire through every inch of it—every fissure and hole in the trunk, fifty meters up, every broken limb shows a hollow darkness and soot blasted out of the tree's center in black rays. I tip my head back in the warm sunlight and shiver.

Working

Two measuring tapes laid end-to-end. Two people to hold them against the trunk. Two other people placing bets off to the side. Three hundred and seventy-four centimeters. I drive a three-inch aluminum nail holding a numbered tag into the tree's bark with the heel of my hand. Like sticking a tack into corkboard. I thump the tree's resonant trunk several times; it's hardly scientific, but I'm pretty sure sequoias like this, just like I'm pretty sure Western junipers are always itchy and like to be scratched.

Lunch Break

This is the thing: working here, I'm always at home. The office converts into a dining room in the time it takes to locate a backrest and establish a patch of dappled shade. We dig out scuffed pears, caprese salads, yogurt with blueberries, last night's lasagna, chocolates to pass around; dig heels into the duff and lean happily against the trees. It's ordinary and comfy, reflexive. Doesn't everyone have a two-thousand-year-old tree for a couch, a carpet that's fun to set smoking with a hand lens, a face smeared with sunscreen and sweat and soot, and a need to keep one eye on that squirrel who's been throwing down cones for the past half-hour? Doesn't everyone understand how a piece of chocolate can be the most important thing that's happened all day?

Fall

Autumn in the Sierra is a stolen season. Small storms wander through and brush the mountains with snow, then the sun thrums back and melts it all. Leaves burnish; needles glisten in washes of light. Quiet in the woods: the sound of moving air, a few blue jay calls, the clock-clocking of the ravens who now travel everywhere in pairs. No visitors; ourselves snuck up into the slopes with extra blankets and a weather eye. An uncertainty, the season at a shifting tilt, but we're snug in the pocket of a warm golden day, then another. Spent ferns mashed bronze along the creek banks. An abundance of twittering small birds and keeled fir seeds twirling down onto the forest floor, the wilting lupine, the dogwood raging red and gold like quiet flames under the big trees. The breeze comes in sweet chomps, the light slants, clouds roll in quietly, and we see breaths.

Snugged thick in a heaven of quilts, in a tent full of flashlight and books, outside October gloams low in the trees, the clouds wipe their hands on the ground, and the leaves drip. Cold and colder and the clouds dissolving into stars, the freeze coming, the earth wet in its dews and breathing mists into clothes and hair. But my small shelter wraps a jolly mulled warmth of high-piled down and cast-off sweaters. Drips on the fly, and well-being humming at every pore.

One Vast Permanence

Keith Ekiss

Before long, I'm down in the valley floor, hiking through the appropriately named Lithodendron ("stone tree") Wash among a diverse array of petrified wood fragments, many as small and sharp as arrowheads, others solid stumps where a hiker can rest. Already the morning is heating up.

Camels, I remember from my reading, once crossed this landscape, like some caravan from a tale in *The Arabian Nights*. In the mid-1850s, Congress commissioned the army to find a western wagon road to California. Reportedly, the camels held up well, but at the onset of the Civil War, they were dropped for the more traditional horse. The Camel Corps had the right idea: in the desert—even the high desert—water is at a premium any time of year, but especially in August.

I've set my sights on a ridge on the opposite side of the valley from where I started, the Black Forest. On top of the ridge, I spot what I had hoped, but didn't expect, to find: the remains of a petrified log that stretches out to a distance of forty feet. The tree is fragmented into sections, but it's stayed close together. It's clearly one tree. And it's two hundred million years old. I'd been to the Grand Canyon many times as a child, and I understand how the sedimentary layers mark geologic time. But a tree that was once living and breathing, a home for birds, with leaves that moved in the wind just like a tree would today? This telescopes time for me in a way that I've never experienced. The land beneath my feet was once equatorial forest. With all the changes on the planet over the ages, it's still fundamentally the same planet.

What, exactly, is petrified wood? The petrified trees in the park are all from extinct species, Triassic conifers. The petrification process has contingencies, you need a number of things in place, namely: trees, a river, and an active volcano. Downed trees find their way into the silt of a river, where the silica from volcanic ash layers through the water and into the cellular structure of the logs, gradually replacing those cells with quartz crystals. The result is alchemical: wood turned into incredibly dense stone. In fact, only topaz, ruby, sapphire, and diamond are harder than petrified wood.

The petrified trees have no rings, in keeping with a landscape that two hundred million years ago had no seasons and was continually humid. Due to platonic shift, the area was previously somewhere in the Atlantic Ocean between South America and Africa. It's come a long way over a long, long time.

Not wanting to test my limits, and knowing how quickly heat stroke and its disorientation can occur, I head back toward the cabin. Stopping for a quick drink of water and to rest in the shade of a large rock, I look up to see that the stone is filled with petroglyphs: images of snakes, lizards, suns, and geometric patterns etched with stone into the rock. A large, wide hand— no, probably a paw, bear paw. A human hand, but with seven fingers. Their presence is a shock. I knew that people once lived here, and in terms of geological time, not that long ago—the last permanent settlements ending around AD 1400. But I wasn't prepared for how fresh these petroglyphs seem.

I came here for the solitude of writing, but already I'm finding myself drawn to the human communities that inhabit, and have inhabited, the park. If I hustle back, I can make it in time for lunch and tell T. Scott Williams, the park's museum curator, what I found, and learn more.

I haven't made a discovery. Scott knows the exact rock I've seen.

"You're finding things," he says, "That's good." What's new for me, it turns out, is just Scott's backyard. "*Tapamveni.* That's the Hopi word for 'rock art.'"

No one's exactly sure, he tells me, what the symbols mean. There's no Rosetta stone decoder, no legend like on a map. One thing's certain: most experts agree that the marks are not simply a matter of where to find water, game, or places to avoid bears. The people who lived here would've already known these facts in intimate detail. Why write what's obvious?

The latest theory is that many of the markings may have had shamanic intent—prayers for healing, in some cases. Most of the petroglyphs were placed to face the sun to receive maximum exposure during the day. If the sun was a god, they wanted him to see their prayers for as long as possible.

Scott opens a cabinet and brings out the smallest clay pot I've ever seen. Thumb-sized. His best guess is that it was made either for or by a child. It's hard to imagine it had a practical use. He shows me a miniature black-and-white effigy of a coyote. It looks decorative, like a toy.

"I can't believe everything they did had a religious purpose," he says. "They had time to make art."

A photographer and geologist by training, Scott spends his days leading tours for schools, conducting outreach programs, and promoting the park. He doesn't fit my preconceptions of a ranger—I expect a grizzly beard, but Scott looks like he'd be as comfortable playing guitar in an alternative rock band as discussing the importance of trilobite fossils. His office is filled with cabinets holding every kind of artifact from the park's history.

"Check this out," he says, opening a cabinet that contains meticulously ordered samples of plant fossils. The pattern of a prehistoric fern lies embedded in a rock so perfectly that I don't need an explanation. It looks like an artist painted the design directly onto it.

"Have you heard about Gertie?" Scott asks. Gertie is a recent discovery—the name given to an ancestor of the dinosaurs that would come to rule the world (and children's books) for the next 150 million years. Gertie, as near as paleontologists can tell, is the first dinosaur on record in North America. Scott slides back a drawer that contains her remaining bones.

I'm clearly underwhelmed, and Scott anticipates the reaction. "It's amazing what the paleontologists can conclude from this." A smattering of vertebrae, a portion of jaw. It took more than science, I think, to reconstruct this carnivore. It took imagination.

"Hold this," Scott says, placing what looks like a pellet-sized piece of charcoal in my hand. It's heavier than I expect for its small size. "Phytosaur scat," he says. "Two hundred million years old. High school students love this part of the tour." He's right, it's a thrill to touch the poop, now solid as a bullet, from this Triassic-era alligator. *What rough beast slouched out of the swamp,* I think, *and shat this?*

There's a tension here, ever present, between permanence and erosion. Because there's no longer any river, no new silt is being deposited. Despite the hardness of the petrified wood, the landscape is gradually eroding. The park was founded with the mission of protecting the fragile environment and the treasure trove of exposed petrified wood, but visitors have stolen untold examples, hauling out the wood by the truckload, or piece by piece in backpacks and purses. *Who will miss one piece?* they must think.

Photographs reveal the decimation. In the early days,

when the park was still a national monument, the reserves of petrified wood were vastly larger. The park has grown increasingly vigilant about protecting its resources, stopping cars at checkpoints to search for artifacts, and offering amnesty for the return of stolen items. In fact, many of these thieves have voluntarily mailed the pilfered wood back, feeling a hefty sense of guilt, if not an outright curse, at the bad luck that befalls them the moment they leave the park and pop a tire on the interstate. The park displays copies of their guilt-ridden apologies; there are hundreds of such letters.

A piece of petrified wood, about the size of a baby's fist, sits on my writing desk in the adobe cabin—built by the Civilian Conservation Corps in the mid-1930s—where I stay. My parents, upright citizens, bought the petrified wood for me as a souvenir, where others might have stolen it, on a trip to the park in 1974, when I was six years old. It has all the solidity and otherworldliness of a meteorite. The fragment retains the remnants of what looks like hardened bark, whitened with age to the color of dirty birch. This is rare. The natural processes of decay usually means that all branches, twigs, and bark were rubbed off the tree before the petrification process began. Like the phytosaur scat, it's heavier than it looks. Its age seems unfathomable. These trees existed before flowers.

Since childhood, I'd kept the petrified wood in a small box along with a pewter Viking galleon, a few baseball cards, and other mementos. I tried one day to write a poem about this strange treasure, but I couldn't, I realized, because I had no idea how the wood became petrified. A quick search turned up not only the park's website and a fine explanation of the petrification process, but also a note about the park's Artist in Residence program, which was looking for volunteers for its second year. The deadline was in three days.

Why not? I thought, and hastily assembled an application, including an essay about why I wanted to visit the park and a sample of my poems about the desert southwest. A month later, I received a call from Scott. I'd be the first writer to stay in the park as part of the volunteer program. My duties? Simple: learn about the park, write poems, and give a public reading at the end of my two-week stay.

"I'll see you in August," I said.

On mornings when I don't get up early to hike before the onset of the heat, I work at my desk, reviewing the previous day's notes and digital photographs of my walks, the pictures of petroglyphs, shrubs, vistas, lightning. I open the cabin door, move a chair onto the back patio, and start to write, mindful for darkling beetles that try to slip past security into the cabin. I've come to befriend these darkling beetles and count on their company in my solitude. As with any creature, when you first meet, you learn its name. I'm charmed at once, the way "darkling" conjures up the distant, frocked world of Victorian poetry, Thomas Hardy's "The Darkling Thrush." I fool myself and start to think that they enjoy my presence. I find their steadiness, as they creep along the base of the outside wall toward the open door, admirable.

"Don't worry," I tell them, "I'm not a crusher."

Over the next ten days, I spend more time visiting sites that record evidence of human habitation, photographing petroglyphs and speculating on their meaning. I visit the Puerco ruin and the Agate house (built entirely of petrified wood), and I hike the Pipeline Trail, which features a veritable art gallery of every shape, size, and kind of petroglyph imaginable. Although I've come here for solitude, I'm beginning to realize that it's the human presence that will leave its deepest impression.

Other writers have preceded me in this landscape and left

their language as monument. John Muir lived here with his daughter after his beloved wife died, and he named one of the areas Blue Forest. It's poetic, but it's also literally true. Cobalt and chromium give the rock a warm, inviting, blue tone. The closest I've seen to it before is the color of Hopi piki bread, made from blue corn.

Other names similarly advertise their strange wonder: the Jasper Forest, the Crystal Forest, the Agate Bridge. The names, frankly, enchant. The beauty and diversity of the colors are surprising, entrancing. A hyper-orange. A light brown, like coffee when you've poured too much milk into it. The delicate pink of the inside of cottontail ears. All the microtones of the chromatic scale. Georgia O'Keefe, I think, would have felt at home among these gradations of adobe, elephant gray, and blue.

Writers need solitude. But I'll admit that it's lonely at night. With the park closed, the only people nearby are the rangers and park personnel who live near the entrance. I could push things and try to make friends for a couple of weeks, invite myself over for an evening meal, but I get the sense that I'd be intruding on family politics. These people have lived together for a long time in close proximity and without much outside interference; they call themselves "lifers," and I don't want to take sides.

For company, there's a radio station that plays classic rock, more than a few stations with fire-and-brimstone preachers, and, on a few nights, when the atmospheric conditions are perfect for long-distance radio transmission, I can even listen to the baseball games from San Francisco.

On Wednesday, as planned, Scott and I drive out to Mountain Lion mesa, a site he wants to show me for its petroglyphs and evidence of human settlement. Past the Teepees (hills shaped like teepees), we turn off the main road through a locked gate.

This is the privilege of rolling with park personnel that I've been waiting for: ditching the sanctioned tourist spots as we bump along slowly for a few miles down a narrow, cratered dirt road. Within what remains a small national park, there are a remarkable variety of landscapes. Here, we're on the plains, grassy mounds, dry arroyos, and mesas that wouldn't take five minutes to climb. We stop abruptly.

"This is it," he says.

By "it," I'm not entirely clear what he means. A mesa, a floodplain. Even to someone like myself, who loves the desert, it's barren. There's no immediate indication that there's ever been any noteworthy presence here.

"A stream used to run through here," Scott says. "The white-tailed antelope still come out." At the base of the mesa, Scott points to petroglyphs. You could easily walk by and miss them. But once seen, their mystery bears scrutiny.

At times, it's like a comic book on the rock: a goofy antelope with a snout like a rubber hose, behind which a ghost with a spooky 'O' mouth hovers over. A sad, circular face. More bear paws. A Kokopelli jamming on its flute beside the head of a woman. There's a large figure with a spiral for an abdomen. "We call this one the space man," Scott says. "It's the only one that's like it." There's a bird with a man in its beak.

At this point, the mystery has become agonizing. Surely, there's an explanation, but it's probably religion, and if the local ancestors of these inhabitants have the key to what this means, they're not saying.

After a few more minutes of admiring, speculating, and photographing, we work our way to the top of the mesa. There's a cool breeze and a good view of storm clouds far off toward the horizon, lightning zigzagging toward the earth. In the center

of the mesa, rounded mounds of earth I recognize at once—
the remains of dwellings. Beneath the weeds and grass, the
rock walls are clearly visible. I'm not in the middle of nowhere.
People lived here.

"Unexcavated," Scott says. "We don't dig up everything."

The park scientists find new archaeological sites all the time;
there are close to a thousand in the park, but there isn't the time
or the money to dig up each one. Beyond that, there's a sense
of respect. We don't need to learn everything. Last year, when
the remains of a human skeleton were found, there was a lot of
negotiation and paperwork with the local tribes. Navajo, Hopi,
and Zuni descendants all have a claim to this land, its history,
and the remains of its people. With respect comes a certain
amount of bureaucracy.

At my feet, there's seemingly no end to the number of black-
and-white pottery shards. They're everywhere. The bowl broke,
and that was it—returned to the earth. Over the side of one
cliff, Scott shows me a midden where refuse was thrown.

"It's like they left last week," I say, although it was likely over
six hundred years ago when the last permanent settlements
moved on for reasons that aren't exactly clear. Lack of water?
Change in climate? We tend to project our current problems
back in time. The land shows evidence of continuous human
habitation for nine hundred years; the park's been here for less
than a hundred years. It will take a lot of effort to preserve its
story for as long as people once lived here.

On my last night in the park, before returning to San Francisco,
I have trouble sleeping. It's a windy evening, and the park
has become colder at night. It's now September, and fall is
approaching. Three or four times, waking me from sleep, I hear
the distinct sound of clawing at my cabin door, a deliberate,
intentional scratching. It can't be the sound of the wind; the
rhythm is too exact.

I'm not superstitious. I don't believe in ghosts, and I'm a borderline atheist, but when I open the door, nothing's there. No animal, no tumbleweed, no sight of anything. A park ranger's practical joke? Unlikely. I'd hear their approach or retreat. Would an animal be so deliberate? What kind of animal? Why would it leave and come back?

My thoughts zip to my friend Mimi and her stories of the Navajo spirit who appears on roads in the dark and causes cars to turn over into ditches.

What's making that sound? No explanation satisfies my fears.

Eventually, I fall asleep for good. At night, whoever is out there, the desert is theirs again.

Days in Paradise

Nathan Rice

I

It goes like this: Wake up at 5:45 AM. Roll off the bunk. Don the kitchen uniform: black-and-white checked pants; starched, white polyester collared shirt; greasy, old shoes; white apron; and green ball cap. Stumble downstairs to the kitchen. Say groggy good-mornings to sleepy cook staff and pour a cup of coffee. Stand behind the cook line and stare at the empty, shining kitchen: the reflection of fluorescent lights on the stainless steel counter, the eerie, precious quiet in this usually chaotic space.

Now take stock. It's either hazy in the head from last night's dormitory festivities, or stiff and pleasantly sore from yesterday's hike/climb/ski, or a combination of the two. Hope that Stacy doesn't start blasting her favorite thrash-metal from the food-splattered boom box.

Flip on the steam table and flattop grill. Wake the deep fryer from its coagulated sleep. Let caffeine clear the cloudy mind and prepare for the tedious tasks at hand. With luck, a prep list will materialize out of the haze—important, time-sensitive details that easily evaporate in the thin, pre-dawn air. Early in the season it's scribbled on grease-stained roller paper:

1 tub green peppers diced
1 tub red peppers diced
2 tubs onion diced
1 tub green onion garnish
5 tubs cheese
12 flats of eggs

And so on. (Later in the season, the list is lost and you hope you don't forget something.)

Ignore the clock for now; just stay busy. Enjoy the grace period, the cold embrace of the walk-in fridge. Pull up the apron like a basket and fill with vegetables. Peppers are easy chopping. Onions are no fun. Stock up the omelet side of the line. Now look at the clock.

6:34.

Initiate countdown.

Get a bag of eggs from the walk-in—the bulging, two-gallon sack full of viscous, homogenized, apricot-colored liquid, presumably containing real eggs in some undisclosed proportion. This is not what you think of when you order "scrambled" off the menu. Pour plenty of oil on the now-hot flattop and let fly the sunny goo from the bag's plastic spout. A satisfying sizzle peels off the flattop and the liquid spreads out over the hot surface until there is a four-foot square of hot, bubbling egginess to tame. With a large steel spatula, reign in the far edges of the egg field, folding the cooked underside back to center. Keep it moving with sweeping, fluid strokes of spatula and molten egg. *Chop chop* with the edge of the tool, toss it around and then pile it, slightly undercooked, in a hotel pan on the steam table. Cover and let rest.

Now for hash browns. They come embalmed in a half-gallon waxed-paper carton about one-quarter full of hard, dehydrated slivers of spud. Add hot water until two-thirds full. Close and wait 15 minutes. Come back and the carton is brimming with hot, shredded potatoes, like the same small miracle that transformed those magic toy tablets of childhood into strange, gooey dinosaurs of unknown origin. Throw the rehydrated spuds on the flattop with plenty of oil and serve with salt and pepper to taste.

Breakfast is served at Mount Rainier National Park, Paradise, Washington. It's seven o'clock, and the dining-room doors are open. And really, for a restaurant at 5,400 feet—stuck on the side of the tallest volcano in the Lower 48—it has a pretty good menu. "Denny's in the sky," a coworker used to joke. But Denny's doesn't have buffalo stew. Or huckleberry pie.

The whine of the first order ticket in the printer is the starting gun. By seven-thirty, it won't quit. What ensues is a futile attempt to defy the second law of thermodynamics, which states that ordered systems will inevitably succumb to disorder. Entropy will prevail. Eggshells will fly. Over-easy yolks will break and be hurled across the line from hot pan to trash (with luck). The time you need will speed up while the time you want to pass will slow down.

By ten o'clock the place is a mess, the masses are fed, our faces are covered with oil and sweat, and the work is temporarily done. I untie my apron, toss it on the counter, grab a bowl of lukewarm oatmeal, add raisins, brown sugar, walnuts, and cream, and walk out into the morning.

The air is so brisk and sweet it stops me, bowl in hand, at the threshold. I close my eyes and breathe in the complex perfume of fir, snow, and every wildflower out there, and I am renewed. I open my eyes to see the summit of Rainier floating 9,000 feet above in the powder-blue ether, painted yellow in the high morning light. I sit and eat my oatmeal in paradise.

This is why I am here. Not for the meager paycheck or the redeeming culinary servitude. I'm here to live and play in the mountains, to get to know this alpine wonderland in whose shadow I was born and raised, on the shores of Puget Sound. Paradise—my home for the summer—sits just below tree line. This mammoth volcano is my backyard.

The lunch shift goes about the same, and then after a noble attempt to clean up the aftermath of eggshells, burger buns, and scatter-shot penne, I clock out and retreat to my dorm room.

It's three o'clock. I trade grease-stained polyester for worn-out Gore-Tex. I stuff my daypack, strap my skis to it, and evacuate the lodge.

Five minutes later, I'm trudging up the trail to Camp Muir. Wildflowers the spectrum over surround—the whole R-O-Y-G-B-I-V and then some represented by Indian paintbrush, tiger lily, monkey flower, hellebore, lupine, gentian, and silky phacelia, respectively. The alpine air is honey-thick with the sun-warmed syrup of their blooms. The hulking mass of Mount Rainier lumbers above, its reddish, volcanic foundation encased in blue-white glaciers: The Nisqually, the Kautz, and the high shoulder of the Ingraham are the only immediately visible of its twenty-six glaciers, its thirty-five square miles of permanent ice.

The Nisqually Glacier tumbles down the mountain in freeze-frame, roaring by at a pace of some eighteen inches per day. Unseen, falling seracs thunder down the icefall in the warm afternoon. With its mighty weight, the glacier carves out the gorge a thousand feet below and sends its silty, roiling meltwater all the way to the salty Puget Sound, about 80 miles west.

The Puyallup tribe who have lived under this beastly mountain for thousands of years named it Tacobet, or "Mother of All Waters," in a rough translation from their Twulshootseed language. The Yakima tribe to the east and other tribes called it Tahoma. In 1792, Captain George Vancouver—an early explorer of Puget Sound who, from his tall ship, was allegedly the first

European to lay eyes on the shimmering white mound—named the mountain after his friend Rear Admiral Peter Rainier, who died on the journey and never actually saw the peak. The European habit of naming mountains after men never made sense to me, despite the accidental appropriateness of Rainier (the average annual rainfall of the park is 140 inches). The name Tahoma, with its cultural and ecological context, rings truer.

The remains of winter's snow gradually creep up the mountain as summer wears on. Early in the season, I can ski all the way back to the parking lot—a delightful, thigh-killing, 4,600-foot descent. These midsummer days, the snow starts at around 6,800 feet on Panorama Point.

I turn and face south to see the earth drop away. The vast expanse of rolling, emerald timberland unfolds beyond. The Tatoosh Range forms an east–west rampart of minor peaks: Unicorn, Castle, Pinnacle, Plummer, Denman, Lane, Wahpenayo, Chutla, Eagle. Farther south, the bulky Mount Adams volcano rises triumphant into the blue sky, contrasting with the blown-out crater of Mount Saint Helens to the west. The clear air even allows the distant white cone of Oregon's Mount Hood to join the scene, affording over a hundred miles of line-of-sight visibility—a rare occasion in this land of rain and clouds.

I turn back to the slope, my head down, and trudge upward again, fighting gravity, burning thighs to earn those sweet turns back down the mountain.

II

Doug bursts through the door after his dinner shift, big climbing pack strapped to his back. Mine's already on, and at 9:00 PM we are off. Our headlamps light the way as we weave through the darkened meadows up to the Muir Snowfield. Clouds have rolled in, and a light drizzle falls as we ascend toward Camp Muir where Rob, Jim, and Annie—our other climbing partners—are likely asleep in their tent. The wind picks up as we top out on Panorama Point. I fight a creeping sense of doubt; we maintain a noble silence on the subject. The weather is the belligerent elephant in the swirling room of clouds. Nervous energy quickens our pace as we kick steps up the snowfield.

Sooner than expected, my pack grows heavy. The drudgery of another 2,500 feet of wet elevation starts to set in. I stop and breathe. A faint glow is lighting up the clouds around us, and the gray pall above seems darker somehow. I keep on, and in another fifty feet, the shroud of clouds strips away and we are bathed in full moonlight. Our whispered exclamations are the only sound.

"Did you know it's a full moon tonight?"

"No idea. We got lucky."

The whole mountain now glows in a muted blue brilliance, rendering headlamps obsolete. The peak takes on a whole new character in the moon's steely spectrum—darker shadows, pitch-black crevasses, more space for the imagination to fill in the blanks. We continue on with heightened morale and gape at the bright, white sea of clouds below us, stretching out to the obscure horizon.

Another thousand feet up, we stop for water. As I gaze up toward Camp Muir, trying in vain to gauge the distance, I notice a strange shimmering in the night sky just above Anvil Rock. I'm not sure if I actually see anything, but then it streaks again, unmistakable. Green ribbons of light undulate up into the darkness and then disappear. I'm dumbstruck. My eyes water at the pure beauty of it, at my total lack of reference for what it could be.

"Doug," I croak. He doesn't hear me. "Doug, what the hell is that?" My voice quakes.

"Whoa. What—?"

It suddenly occurs to me. "Northern lights?"

A long, quiet pause.

"Yeah, it's gotta be." Another streak of green light sweeps upward and wavers in the field of stars. Hot tears on my face turn cold in the wind. I am dumb with awe. No longer in a hurry, we continue up, stopping frequently to absorb the beauty of the mountain night.

By midnight, after a brief nap at Camp Muir, we are packed, roped up, and ready to start climbing the remaining 14,410 feet to the summit. A frigid wind blows down over Gibraltar Rock and whistles through my helmet; I'm eager to get moving. It is cold and clear, and the beaming moon lights the way. Doug leads out across the head of the Cowlitz Glacier toward Cadaver Gap. I wait for the forty feet of rope between us to play out and then follow, each step *clink*ing the carabiners and pulleys on my harness, the methodical *chink* of ice axe on hard snow. Rob, Annie, and Jim make their own rope team behind us.

Navigating across glaciers in the dark is done carefully. It takes a combination of keen awareness, knowledge of glacial behavior, and dead reckoning, with ice axe as divining rod, to detect chasms of space underfoot—snow-covered crevasses that frequently swallow climbers. I'm secretly glad to let Doug take the lead.

We move steadily through Cadaver Gap and across the flats of the Ingraham Glacier.

Rockfall tumbles echoing down from the volcanic layer-cake of Gibraltar Rock. Hulking blocks of ice, seracs, lean over us, menacing. Reaching Disappointment Cleaver, we remove our crampons, coil the ropes, and begin the long trudge up the rotten volcanic rock ridge that takes us around the Ingraham Icefall and to the more mellow glacier above. Moving through this otherworldly icescape in darkness is unnerving. Hazards abound and, despite trying to discern them out of darkness, all we can do is focus on our own spheres of visibility and keep moving, thanking the moon for its dim, pale light.

An hour later, we are on top of Disappointment Cleaver and ready to get back on the ice. Annie is feeling the altitude, so we wait a cold twenty minutes and rest. She pukes, sick with altitude, lack of oxygen. She can't keep going. Rob wisely brought a stove and sleeping bag for such an occasion. They unrope and bundle up, graciously sending us onward. The weather is clear, and they can descend together if need be. Doug, Jim, and I make a rope team, don our crampons, and continue on up in silence, ice crunching underfoot with each step, the hissing of the stove fading behind us.

By three in the morning, we are at 12,500 feet—less than 2,000 feet from the summit. The eastern horizon is painted with a pale blue light, gradually morphing into yellows and oranges as the sun creeps up from the other side. Between moondown and early dawn, we barely need headlamps. We weave through gaping crevasses now made visible in the predawn light, their depths measured in color from a light aquamarine to a dead dark blue to a black that turns the gut. Seracs of bizarre geometry rise frozen around us, prickling with crazy arrays of icicles. We are well above any outcrops of rock that might remind us we are still attached to the ground. All is snow and ice.

Our pace slows with each step as precious oxygen molecules become scarcer in the high air. Deep breaths. Left foot. Right foot. Rest. When climbing starts to feel like suffering, I remind myself that I won't remember this part—that the pain will fade quickly and the beauty will endure.

We make slow progress up the ice cap, hope-inspiring false summits revealing themselves with each switchback. The vast landscape below is obscure in the early light; my compromised mindset can't grasp the scale. All concentration is consumed by walking, breathing.

The eastern sky is now an unfathomable orange, a vermillion aurora that defies language. Words are useless when it's painted across the sky. There is only the cold, quiet radiance. The slow, methodical pace becomes a meditation. Release the mind. Breathe deep. Ingest the moment. Keep walking.

Time loses hold in the thin air. We finally arrive on the crest of crater, the volcanic crucible that made all 14,410 feet of mountain under our feet. Shards of wind-scoured ice stab skyward as we walk slowly, our eyes on the high mound on the other side. I am queasy with altitude and bewildered.

A final push up the pumice earth of the crater rim and we are finally there: the Columbia Crest, the true summit of Mount Rainier, at last. We share exhausted embraces, our smiling faces frozen in the cold air. There is almost no wind.

With the bowl of the crater in the foreground, we face east and watch the sun slowly rise from under distant clouds, the glowing orb somehow distorted into an oval through layers of atmosphere. It finally cracks through the cloud layer like the primordial, cosmic egg that made the world and spills brilliant light across the land. Sulfurous vapors emanating from the crater's edge light up pink in the new day.

The scale of our elevation blows out any sense of reference. The Tatoosh peaks are barely discernible on the far-flung plane of the earth below. The only relevant landmarks are Mount Adams and Mount Saint Helens to the south, and Glacier Peak and the distant, white beacon of Mount Baker to the north, marking the Cascadian spine of volcanoes that stretches far beyond, a small arc in the pan-Pacific "Ring of Fire." The craggy, purple tooth of Mount Stuart juts out to the northeast. A blue haze to the west is the vast body of ocean. Obscure, twinkling lights in the mountain's dark shadow miles below must be Seattle.

We are on top of the world.

III

I'm walking back to my room drenched from head to toe in French-toast batter. While enjoying my post-work cup of coffee on the back stoop, gazing at peaks, I was ambushed and doused in three gallons of frigid, thirty-five-degree batter. As the hot sun slowly cooks the eggy goo onto my skin, the walk home gives me time to ponder revenge.

A couple of weeks later, it is John the sous chef's birthday, and time to strike.

My carefully concocted plan is for Ned to take John out back to have a smoke. Tim has egg batter and I have flour. John will be breaded. Giddy, I coax Tim ahead of me and out the back door. My first look at John tells me something is wrong. He has a soup pot in his hand and a lit cigarette sticking out of a big, wily grin. Tim spins around to empty the egg on my head. I duck.

Then, scripted, John douses me in flour.

Now I am the breaded one, prepped for the deep fryer, and it is on. John gets one look at my battered-up face and bolts, cackling with glee. I chase after him and flour him, along with most of the stoop.

An unfortunate turn of events it was, but I harbor a secret weapon. Fish sauce is the nastiest foodstuff in the entire kitchen inventory: a terrible, brown, liquid concoction made from reduced fish parts. The stuff smells like death itself. A teaspoon, but no more, brings to life a coconut-curry sauce like nothing else. Conveniently for my purposes, it comes in a squeeze bottle.

I dust off, go inside, and congratulate them on their ruse, the filthy traitors. I let the excitement dissipate for ten minutes or so and then I grab the bottle of death sauce from the reach-in fridge. As John comes around the corner to the line, a stream of brown fish goo greets him in the chest.

"Aw! You bastard!" he yells and retreats.

IV

There are six of us, freshly clocked out from work and winding down Paradise Road to Reflection Lakes in Ned's old Ford truck. From there, trails up the Tatoosh peaks cut through subalpine forest and tarns, then up to the alpine and the chossy, volcanic crest of the range. By some unimaginable geologic process, this ridge used to be the crater of the mountain. A story goes that native guides led the first Mount Rainier climbing expedition up and over the Tatoosh in an attempt to wear them down and sabotage the effort. Perhaps they feared the consequences of mortal men treading on their lofty god.

The snowy couloir gets steep as we pass through the portal leading to higher ground. The late-season snow is hard, requiring ice axes, but the creek beneath the snow has melted an unseen cavern beneath us, threatening neck-deep postholes. We move cautiously upward.

We are aiming for Unicorn Peak with its spiry namesake of a summit. I wonder what the Puyallup call it—what that old way of knowing, which still hangs like mist on the land, could show us beneath the thin veneer of new European place names.

Now Tim and I wait for the rest to catch up. Eventually, we are all back in the sun, eyeing the final snowfield leading to the crest. It's one more precious, sunny day in the shadow of Tahoma.

In an hour, we are all standing below the final summit pitch, an easy but consequential thirty-foot climb up the horn of Unicorn Peak. We spot each other from below, words of encouragement swallowed in the expansive relief around us.

Soon we are standing on top, triumphant. High-fives are slapped around. The earth drops away on all sides. Rainier in its hugeness is lit up pink by the setting sun, distant glaciers painted mauve. The rest of the Tatoosh Range stretches west toward the sun, toward the sea. Three thin clouds populate the western sky, illuminated in an impossibly vivid ochre-pink that hovers there beyond description.

Receding snow patches make strange jigsaw shapes in the dark shadows of the ridge below. Snowmelt gathers into gushing streams in the valley a thousand feet down, bolstering the perpetual background roar of falling water. Lush meadows crowd the meandering alpine stream. Even way up here, the air is sweet with flowers. A bird alights on a nearby rock and tilts its head toward me.

It's like a punch in the gut, all of this beauty. How—*why*—is this world so utterly beautiful? After living up here all summer, my mind has been rewired in the mountain's presence, better adapted to perceive such boundless grace, and still I can't fathom it. So I stop thinking and let my senses do the work.

The sun is swallowed by horizon. The mountain glows in silence. And an answer slowly unfolds.

No reason. The world is beautiful for no reason.

I feel weak and faint-headed, like in freefall. I bow my head to the earthly phenomena that ground us in this paradise.

The bird flits off into the void.

Never Lost

Elizabeth Arnold

In the months between my junior and senior year of college, I took a job wrangling at a guest ranch in Wyoming's Bridger-Teton National Forest in Grand Teton National Park. I was hoping for nothing more than the chance to ride some good ranch horses and to live—at least for a while—in a place that claims to be "the last of the great West."

One of my first nights on the ranch, while sitting on the porch of the bunkhouse and looking out into the valley, I watched as the sun disappeared behind the mountains, casting purple shadows across the thick strings of the Buffalo Fork River and the backs of the horses grazing in the lower meadow. I realized in that moment that I would never get tired of the view. No matter how many times I looked out beyond the ranch, the Tetons would always be there, standing behind the river like a promise. And I would always be surprised by how unexpectedly they rose straight and clean out of the valley floor, piercing through thin layers of clouds and cutting into sharp blue sky. In that moment, I knew that this was more than a summer job—that there is a reason people are drawn to this place, to a landscape still wild and powerful.

Just then, Paul, the ranch's fly-fishing guide, walked over to where I sat on the bunkhouse porch with two coffee cups in his hand. He stood tall and rugged, an embodiment of the Marlboro

Man, with a thick, silvered mustache and a worn denim shirt. He handed me a cup and said that the mountains always look better when you're watching them on a spring night over a cup of black coffee. Leaning against the rail of the porch, Paul looked out over the darkening space of pasture and willow beds and quick-moving water. He took a long sip and told me that after ten years in Jackson Hole, he'd never gotten tired of the view, because it always had a way of catching him off guard.

I told him I was stunned when I came down Togwotee Pass after my three-day drive to the ranch. I wasn't embarrassed to tell him that I'd pulled the truck over and stood in the middle of the road awhile, feeling so small, so overwhelmed, looking down at the full spread of the mountains for the first time.

He told me later that evening—when the only sounds on the ranch were the soft and distant bells of horses turned loose—that after coming here for a vacation from a high-pressure job back in Tennessee, this place and the promise of a life spent knee-deep in clear water drew him away from a hundred thousand dollars a year and a pension. "This valley has a way of grabbin' hold of ya and never lettin' go," he said.

I took a long sip. The coffee was almost gone then, and the stars had overtaken the night sky.

In 1825, trapper and explorer Jim Bridger arrived to the Jackson area in search of wealth, Western adventure, and beavers. He spent most of his life learning the intricacies of the region—from the Snake River, Two Ocean Pass, and Gros Ventre Valley to the steep cut of trails carved between the Teton Range and Yellowstone. Bridger knew the paths that would lead him safely over Togwotee Pass or Hoback Junction as he traveled along Jackson's trapping and trading routes.

But the life of a mountain man is a solitary one, with only a horse, a few mules, and the wide space of a rough and ruthless landscape for company. The promise of seclusion in new and beautiful country—a promise that drew so many westward—was often the very thing some were unprepared for. The isolation, the feeling of being so alone yet surrounded by inexplicable grandeur, was almost too much to handle for many early homesteaders and those who unsuccessfully tried their hands at living off the land and trapping. Some were simply overcome by the loneliness; others fell prey to a land unafraid of showing newcomers they didn't belong.

But Bridger found a way to make peace with the land. Perhaps he was the sort who found solace in the openness, in the inexplicable power and draw of a landscape capable of destroying him if he let it. He was able to make a life in the mountains, to form a partnership with them that allowed him to become one of the most regaled and respected trappers of the Rocky Mountain Fur Company.

Bridger's prowess for mountain living made him and his notorious tall tales famous among other trappers and guides. He liked to tell campfire stories of "petrified birds who sang petrified songs." His skill and intimate knowledge of the Teton and Rocky mountain ranges made him an invaluable asset to explorers and developers.

In 1850, a man asked Bridger to find a shorter route across the Rockies than the South Pass. Bridger showed him to a path that led past the Great Basin and would soon come to be known as Bridger's Pass. The route was first put to use as an overland mail route; later it would become Union Pacific Railroad tracks. It still functions today as part of I-80.

The valley has probably not changed much since Bridger and the early homesteaders moved here, to this rare place of canyons, sage plains, creeks, rivers, and deep, dense timber. Today it is no longer just mountain men and homesteaders who are drawn to Jackson Hole. Today people come to forget life and to experience life at the same time. They come to take part in a landscape larger than they are, a landscape they can get lost in for a little while.

Grand Teton National Park—occupying Jackson Hole valley's northwestern reaches—beckons modern adventurers. In winter they arrive to ski and snowmobile. In summer they come to hike the trails around the Tetons and the many lakes that sit at the base of the mountains. They come to fly-fish the Buffalo Fork River and ride horseback into the backcountry with seasoned wranglers and outfitters. They come to camp out in a place of raw, unfettered wilderness and to raft, canoe, or kayak down the Snake River. And a few of the bravest attempt to climb all menacing 13,770 feet of the Grand Teton.

Lynette came to the ranch to decide what to do about her husband. A striking woman in her late forties, she told me this as I adjusted her stirrups and as Blackjack—her mount for the week—nosed my elbow. I hoped that Blackjack was telling me that he would be nice to Lynette, because the week before he'd had a lady from south Texas, and he kept ramming her knees into the trees along the trail. I'd hear the sweet little blonde with bruised knees let out tiny groans and sighs every few strides behind me. And so I would turn in my saddle and smile at her, tell her to rein him away from the trees, to use her legs and hands to steer. And she would just say, in her sweet little Texas drawl, "Ah honey, old Blackjack's just fine. He's not doin' it on purpose."

I didn't have the heart to tell her that yes, actually, he was. That old Blackjack would much rather be back in the corral, eating hay, than carrying her along the willow draw ride for the fourth time this week.

So I hoped Blackjack would be nice to Lynette, and I wished that the head wrangler had chosen another horse for her, because she seemed like the type of person who deserved a nice horse—a horse that wouldn't ram her knees into trees.

It was late in the day, and the color of the sky around the Tetons had started to take on the orange, hazy hues of early evening. The temperatures had begun to dip a little. The ride with Lynette was my last for the day. She seemed comfortable as she sat aboard Blackjack, not saying anything else, just waiting for me to make sure everything was in order.

As a wrangler, it was my job to make sure that the stirrups were adjusted evenly and fit the length of the rider's leg, that the cinch holding the saddle in place was tight, that the rider knew how to hold the reins correctly. Lynette's firm grip on the reins and upright seat made me think she had ridden before. Her short brown hair swung loose around her face, and her straw Stetson—which I was certain she'd bought just for the trip—did not seem as out of place on her as it did on most other guests.

Lynette was staying alone at the ranch for a month. Both of these things were a little unusual. Most of our guests came with their families. We also had newlyweds, dating couples, and the occasional group of old friends. But hardly anyone came alone, and almost no one stayed more than a week. As we wranglers combed through a hundred acres of pasture in search of 150 horses at five in the morning, we didn't have much to talk about, aside from where all the horses were hiding, what Rick the cook was going to make for breakfast, and the bits of gossip we picked up about the guests. So I had heard that Lynette was at the ranch alone, but I didn't know why.

I swung across Scotch's back, and with Lynette and Blackjack following, we moved off past the corrals, past the cabins, past the woodshed, and onto the trail that would lead us into the mountains behind the ranch. I looked over my shoulder to make sure Lynette was behind me and saw her leaning over Blackjack's neck, twisting her fingers in his long mane. I could hear her talking to him, telling him what a beautiful horse he was, what a beautiful ride we were going to have. Her enthusiasm made me smile and reminded me of all the reasons why I loved my job.

The first time I rode down along the river trail alone, it was late in the day, after the other wranglers and I had finished our task of fixing the fence line along the south edge of the big pasture. The first guests would be arriving the next week, and we were told to spend the rest of the day out on the trails, making sure we were ready to start guiding on them.

As I came upon the river, I let my horse step knee-deep into the flowing water and dip her muzzle into the roiling flow of it. I felt as though I'd come out here and found something I never even knew was missing.

I felt content every morning, when the Tetons greeted me from the bunkhouse porch, and yet was constantly challenged by a landscape I was so unfamiliar with, so intensely in awe and fear of at the same time. Yet I knew the chance to share this place with other people—to take them to these new places I was learning about—was somehow worth the challenge. I'd go along with them and ride steadily up and through sage plains dotted with yellow monkey flowers and tender, purple shooting stars. I'd take them across swift, shallow creeks or to the trail that ran down along the river and spilled out into groves of aspen where the wind shifted between the leaves in a way that was both welcoming and warning, shushing you into keeping the secrets they told as they quaked.

Every time I rode off into the mountains on horseback, there was a risk of coming across something I might not know how to handle. Though I had my can of bear spray tethered to my saddle and a radio fixed to my hip, there was always a faint fear of what I was certain this place was capable of unleashing. At times like that, when I was riding alone and a little later than I should have been, and darkness began to set in over the trails, my mind always seemed to go to the training meeting we had with the bear expert.

He was a bearded, burly sort of man who had spent most of his life in the backcountry. I remember asking him what to do about the mountain lions, whether bear spray worked on them. And I still wasn't very secure in the idea that, for the spray to work, you had to be thirty feet away from the bear and in its direct path.

He just said, "Little lady, if those cats want ya, they're gonna get ya. They're stalkin' your every move long before you know they're there."

Even though there was a lot to be afraid of in the park, there was some kind of comfort in knowing that I was surviving. That I was not as afraid as I thought I'd be. Because even though I was always a little uneasy—a little unsure of what I might be getting myself into when I rode down across the river and through the aspen grove as night set in—the beauty of it all, the danger wrapped up in the way the moon began to throw thin, pale fingers of light down over the top of the water as it wound away from the mountains, made me feel a little more at ease. I knew it was the same light that filtered in between the spaces in the trees, between the black-and-white-barked aspens and their tiny leaves, that would soon wave and shush at me as I passed. It was the same light that shifted between the tips of the Tetons, spilled over the slick tin rooftops back at the ranch, and cast pools of light down into the corrals. Though I knew I would lose those beams of light for a few minutes as I passed beyond the aspen grove and up onto the ridge that would lead me back—knew that my heart would quicken, that I'd probably ask my horse to move up into a steady, ground-covering trot— the ranch would always be there, and I knew how to make it back.

It was funny, I thought, that after only a month of riding the trails I had learned my way through the wilderness beyond the ranch, and was more familiar with that harsh country than with any place I'd ever known. My closeness with the land somehow connected me to it, and made me feel safe. Wyoming was a place where the darkness hid real dangers, where fear was more than just a feeling. Since coming to the ranch and riding the trails alone, I had come to understand fear in a real and visceral way. I understood it on those first few rides with the other wranglers when we'd split up in the high country to try to make it down to the ranch by ourselves. Those first solo rides were a way of testing ourselves. Once alone, I would often feel a little lost—sense my chest tightening, my hands sweating around the reins—and struggle to recognize my surroundings. But I began to understand that though my fears were justified, fear wouldn't get me off the mountain. So I would take a deep breath, pat my horse on the neck, and choose a trail I hoped would lead me home.

As my sturdy little horse and I moved through the trees on those first nights alone, I knew that as hard as it had been to pack up my truck and drive west for three days to a job I knew little about in a place I'd only seen in pictures, it would be harder still to pack up and go home to the safety of the life I'd always led.

In 1860—twenty-five years after his arrival in the Jackson area—Jim Bridger was leading an expedition of eastern scientists and government surveyors up from the Wind River Range, through Jackson Hole, and on toward the headwaters of the Yellowstone River. It was late May, and many of the mountain slopes were still entrenched in deep snow. It was only after a difficult, physically trying push that they were able to move through Union Pass and reach the Continental Divide. The party, at Bridger's lead, finally reached the outskirts of Jackson Hole, in the Gros Ventre Fork Valley.

It was here that Bridger became disoriented. There were several routes he could have taken to reach the Yellowstone headwaters. He must have been familiar with the Mt. Leidy Highlands, Togwotee Pass, and Two Ocean Pass—yet he did not try to take these already-established trading routes. A man on the expedition remarked that Bridger seemed "more at a loss than I have ever seen him."

After attempting several other routes unsuccessfully and losing a man beneath the swift spring current of the Snake River, Bridger made a final attempt to find their destination. He was able to lead the men over Teton Pass, but the expedition failed to ever locate the Yellowstone headwaters.

Perhaps the heavy snow had changed the landscape. Perhaps the passage of years spent isolated and alone had affected Bridger's memory. Even after all that time in this wilderness, trapping beaver and successfully making a life from the harsh land, it seems as though Bridger became overwhelmed, lost in the place he knew so well.

There was a joke amongst the wranglers at the ranch that a wrangler is never lost. We enjoyed sharing it with guests not if, but when we lost our bearings in the midst of the endless maze of trails that connects the mountain paths, meadows, canyons, creeks, and lookouts behind the ranch. The trails all seem to double back and twist endlessly over one another. Even though we all knew them—and knew that we just had to find a fence line and then follow it down to get back to the ranch—it was still possible to get a little turned around up there. And so if the guests caught on and noticed that we'd passed the same group of trees, crossed the same creek more than once, we just told them, "A wrangler is never lost."

We'd then say, "Ask me where we are, just ask me." And when they did, we replied, "We're right here."

It was our secret, I suppose, this little joke we had, but it seemed to put people at ease and help them believe we knew exactly what we were doing, knew exactly where we were.

Lynette and I had fallen into a careful, easy rhythm and were far above the ranch, moving through a dense patch of timber high beyond the Buffalo Fork River. She hadn't said anything more about her husband, and I was a little glad for that. I glanced over my right shoulder and watched as she and Blackjack followed. She was speaking to him in quiet, earnest tones, just low enough that I wasn't sure what she was saying. Soft beams of yellow light streamed in through breaks in the evergreen ceiling, letting me know that evening was pressing onward, and that I should be sure to take the shortest route home to the ranch.

A large pine had fallen across the trail in the days since I'd last been through that path, and I turned in my saddle to tell Lynette that we could either go around or let the horses jump over it. She smiled at me and told me she would like to jump. I told her that Blackjack, as lazy as he was, would not take more than a small hop, and that she just needed to balance herself against the horn of the saddle, lean back, push her heels down, and hold on. I went first, letting Scotch break into a trot. He lifted and moved off the ground and over the fallen tree with ease, then shook his head as we landed, proud of himself. I moved him to the edge of the trail and stopped to watch Lynette.

Normally, I wouldn't have done that, allowed a guest the option of jumping fallen timber. Cutting a path around would have been the safer move, but Lynette seemed to appreciate the fact that I'd given her the choice. Just as I expected, Blackjack hopped lazily over our obstacle, his legs barely clearing with an awkward, jarring jump. But Lynette handled it with the grace of someone who'd spent a lifetime in the saddle. She smiled as he landed, and they trotted over to where I sat waiting aboard Scotch.

"That was great," I told her.

She straightened her hat and then leaned down to run her hands over Blackjack's neck, still beaming. "I'm so glad you let me do that," she said.

I smiled back. "No problem. I knew you and Blackjack could handle it."

She sat up, folded her hands, and let them rest on the saddle horn. "You know, my husband would have never wanted me to do that."

I held my smile, not sure what to say.

"He's always worried about me," she added.

I always felt like I never quite knew the right thing to say when people started confiding in me, telling me their stories. I wondered what he thought about her being out there alone. I wondered where he was and what he was doing. But it was not my place to ask those questions. As a wrangler, it was my job to just listen.

The amber light had moved farther down, into the thick spaces between the boughs of the evergreens, and was casting long shadows across the trail and across the horses' necks. So I told Lynette we should probably keep moving.

We pressed forward, guiding the horses along the trail, out of the closeness of the timber and up into the space of a meadow that swept along the eastern edge of a ridge. The ridge cut down to the Buffalo Fork River and was spotted with tufted evening primrose and sagebrush buttercups. Lynette cleared her throat and commented on the beauty of the view from the meadow, and how the sunset was so much more magnificent than any sunset she'd ever witnessed back in Virginia.

There must be something about the space of open country that makes people feel free to share things about the lives they live somewhere else, to say all of the things they somehow feel safe saying from the back of a horse, lost in plains of fescue and sage and wild red Indian paintbrush. Maybe it was the anonymity they felt I held in my position as a wrangler. Maybe the fact that I was out there said something about me, and assured them that their secrets were safe with the stranger riding ahead of them. And maybe they were not actually sharing with me at all, but telling their secrets to a place they knew would not hold onto them, a place that would instead carry them away on prairie winds.

I listened as Lynette told me about her home—a sort of contemporary brick colonial that she and her husband designed themselves after they'd saved enough money. She told me that they decorated it all together as a family, that she and her husband and their daughters spent whole mornings at antique shops and flea markets, picking out trinkets and tchotchkes they felt said something about them as a family. She told me about her job as a publicist, which allowed her enough flexibility to stay at the ranch for a few weeks. She told me about her children: Both girls were now grown and in their last years of college and graduate school. And she told me more about her husband, John, whom she was not sure she was in love with anymore.

"You know, it's funny," she said. "You get married so young, and you think you're so sure, and then all of a sudden, your kids are grown and gone, and it's just the two of you again in this house you've designed and decorated and filled with things that say something about you. And all of a sudden you and this person, this other person, have spent thirty years together, and you're finally alone again. But you feel like you don't even know each other anymore."

She let the silence fall in again for a little while as we wound between the bushes of sweet, heady-scented sage. Blackjack kept putting his head down every few strides, pulling the reins out of Lynette's hands as he tried to grab at the sparse, flaky stems. I turned around and told her to try and beat him to it, to give him a little bump with the reins before he put his head down, that if he knew she was in control, he would stop testing her.

I looked back again and saw her grin as she caught him in the act.

She patted him on the neck and said, "If I were you, if I had the skill you do with horses and came out here at your age . . ." She paused, leaned down to pat Blackjack again, "Well, I don't know if I ever could have gone back."

It was almost dark then, but Lynette didn't seem to mind, and neither did I because the ranch was not too far. The lights from the lodge were small and distant over the edge of the rise we were approaching, and we just had to wind back down into the draw that would lead us to the corrals.

"Do you ever worry about getting lost out here?" Lynette asked.

I twisted in my saddle, with one hand on the reins and the horn, the other on the cantle. Her hat was casting shadows over her face, and it was too dark to meet her eyes. I smiled anyway.

"No, a wrangler is never lost."

Communion

Melanie Dylan Fox

The magnum of cheap merlot in my pack is heavy. The awkward, smooth, green glass thuds against the small curve of my back. My steps fall into a familiar, rhythmic pattern as I follow the trail past the restaurant toward Lower Kaweah, where most of the summer employees live this season. Even though I've followed this trail dozens of times, walking quickly at night is a habit—a remnant of my first season, before I'd learned there was nothing to fear in the darkness.

It's already late. The accounting paperwork at the Lodge dining room took me longer than usual tonight, and I'm not looking forward to spending the evening with my friends. We'll stay up until the first hint of light filters through the trees, drink too much, and tell the same worn-out stories we've told over and over. And the stories will probably remind me too much about the places I still haven't seen during my five seasons here.

But I'm leaving soon, and I have promised to do this one last time. I won this bottle of wine a couple of seasons ago—in a contest among the servers in the Lodge dining room—and have carried it around with me like a burden ever since. During four moves the wine has been wrapped gently with tissue paper, placed in a wooden box, and packed into the back of my station wagon. I've saved it for a special occasion just like this one— possibly the last moment we'll all share together before the season ends.

I come down the dusty hill toward the employee cabins in Lower Kaweah. The air smells like pine needles and stale beer—cheap, canned beer with a watery, metallic taste that promises a bitter headache in the morning. The lights from the nearby hotel are dim, but visible shadows reveal a large group of people who have gathered in the parking lot. I stumble over a small rock in the road. My heart beats faster, and I try not to acknowledge the hollowness tightening and pressing in my chest. After so many summers here I can sense when something is out of place in the forest.

Dozens of people stand in the paved parking lot talking and smoking, some of them with bottles in their hands. Dissonant strains of music come from scattered cabins—stereos blaring heavy metal, bluegrass strummed on an acoustic guitar. An employee whose name I don't know rushes by and I grab his arm.

"What happened? Someone get arrested?" I ask, and I'm only half-joking. Someone getting arrested for public intoxication or for a fistfight has become almost expected. During almost every one of my five seasons in Sequoia National Park, an employee has been seriously injured in an alcohol-related accident. These incidents we keep to ourselves, like shameful secrets.

"Yeah, that guy from the dining room, what's his name? Keith?" Keith is my assistant manager, and I shake my head because my very first thought is that tomorrow is supposed to be my day off.

The tightness in my chest grows stronger. "DUI, the rangers took him down the hill…" My second thought is a split-second image of Keith, drunk, cold, and confused. We had met by chance last winter in a coffee shop, drawn to one another by a passion for writing and mutual grief over our recent failed relationships. When the time came to leave for Sequoia, I managed to convince Keith at the last minute that a season in the forest would provide distance and healing. He is my closest friend here, and no one can tell me where they took him or when he might be back. I sit down on the cold pavement. The employee keeps talking, but I stop listening.

In the thick stacks of photographs from my seasons here, especially the first, so many images share the same conspicuous details: crowds of people smiling and laughing, and somewhere in the photograph—usually displayed proudly—bottles of liquor or drugs. There are photographs of the sequoias and peaks too, but to me those images of nature have become overshadowed by the others. Over the years, I have come to accept that alcohol and drugs are an incongruous part of this seasonal life.

During the height of the summer, more than 400 employees work in Giant Forest, and yet it's still easy to feel alone. Here in Lower Kaweah, I'm surrounded by dozens of acquaintances—all drinking, laughing, and having a good time. Our relationships seem tenuous and superficial, and the shared party experience provides the illusion of intimacy.

Perhaps the constant blur of people moving in and out of our lives makes us hesitant to connect deeply, to ever really know one another. After all, it's common to become close to someone, only to discover that while you slept, he or she quit and left the mountain—virtually disappeared. My first season, I exchanged addresses with everyone, not realizing the artificiality of this gesture; most people I would never see or hear from again.

My first season.

I locked the door to the gift shop and turned toward the sky, hoping for a single strand of moonlight. I had stayed on the phone too long, talking to a friend back home, and the last remaining daylight was gone. I would have to walk home in complete darkness, without a flashlight to guide me.

I followed the Village parking lot lights to the General's Highway, the only road in the park, surrounded by the dense canopy of trees. I was unable to focus my eyes in such darkness. I placed one foot in front of the other, staring straight ahead into nothing. *I've done this before*, I told myself. I knew each twist and bend. Nothing bad would happen.

I turned my body left with a curve in the road and saw a blue light, bouncing in circles between the tall trees. The light was faint, its pattern predictable. The blue was joined by red, and then the white-hot glare of emergency flares. I was still far enough away to see only lights, nothing else, but their meaning was unmistakable.

I turned the final bend in the road and started up the hill toward the employee cabins in Pinewood. Todd, the housing manager, stood in the middle of the road, next to the police car, looking down at the white line reflecting the flashing lights. When I approached, Todd—tired, shoulders slumped—looked up. I finally spoke, not wanting to ask the question that he would have to answer over and over again for a long time.

"What happened?"

Todd took a deep breath. "There's been a really bad car accident." I immediately thought of my friends, my brother. I did not want to ask any more questions. But I needed to know.

"Who? Who is it?"

"Ed from the cafeteria, Julie, and a couple of other people, on their way back up the hill. They were down in Three Rivers playing pool, drinking. The rangers already took Ed away." He paused as if unable to continue. "They don't think he'll make it."

I hadn't known, as I was driving across the country to get here, how much Sequoia National Park would embody the cliché "miles from nowhere." In Giant Forest, where I've worked five seasons, I have access to the usual tourist facilities—cafeteria, gift shops, hotel, and market—and little else. To buy a new book, have a cappuccino, or shop in a dizzyingly large Wal-Mart, I must head south or northeast for at least an hour and a half. Entire days are spent "off the hill" in the dusty, brown foothills of the Sierra Nevada mountains, checking items off the lists my friends give me.

The tourists in Sequoia spend three days, sometimes a week, frantically trying to make up for months of stressful jobs, deadlines, faxes, and e-mails. But few seem able to fully escape. Keith once told me that when he reached the summit of Mount Whitney—the highest point in the contiguous United States—dirty and exhausted after hiking for over a week, the first thing he saw was a man talking on a cell phone.

Those of us who make our home in such isolation have different notions of what it means to escape or get away from it all. Instead of hiking into the backcountry during my days off, I ride roller coasters at Disneyland, visit friends in San Francisco, or read on my favorite beach near Santa Cruz. I want to be where there are more people than trees. Where, instead of silence, I hear the shrill scream of sirens and moving traffic.

When I don't make the trip away from the mountains, I gather with friends after work in someone's cabin. We joke that there's nothing to do here. And nearly always we share these thoughts while passing around a bottle of something: wine, tequila, gin. Or when we need a change of scenery or feel like "going out" for the evening, we head to the Fireside Tavern, the same bar Keith had been drinking in earlier. Through the effects of alcohol and drugs, we search to find the smallest way to ease our physical and emotional isolation.

My second season.

That afternoon, in the employee rec room, I'd leaned back the couch cushions and pulled a blanket around my body. It was still August, but my hands and feet were numb from the unexpected cold weather.

The microwave chimed, and my friend Adam poured clear liquid into the mug from a bottle on the table and handed it to me. I wrapped my hands around the mug, sensation finally coming back into my fingers for the first time in days. The hot chocolate was almost boiling, but I took a sip anyway. The too-sweet taste of peppermint schnapps and milky chocolate was instantly intoxicating. I took three more gulps and wondered if I should slow down—it was only two o'clock in the afternoon.

Adam sat down in the chair next to me. "What do you want to do today?"

I stared into the mug. "I don't care."

"Want me to pick out a movie?" Adam asked.

"I guess. Why don't we wait till Sarah's off work? She'll be done in a couple hours and we can hang out." Sarah, Adam, and I had met at a bonfire party during our first weeks in the park. None of us had arrived with friends and we quickly formed a close circle of companions. In the months since, we were rarely apart and had shared countless hours of laughter and thoughtful conversation.

Adam cleared his throat. "I doubt she'll be back any time soon."

"Huh? What's that mean?"

Sarah had been acting edgy for a while, constantly on the verge of a fight with me. I kept searching my memory for some fragment of conversation or some forgotten moment when I'd annoyed her. I also searched for some way to apologize for whatever it was.

"You don't get it, do you?" Adam shook his head.

"No, I guess I don't." I set down the mug and sat up.

"Crank, Mel. You know, crystal meth." I frowned and shook my head. His expression and voice softened. "She's on speed. Don't you know anyone who does meth?"

I'd come to Sequoia from a small, Midwestern college town. The most that my friends in Indiana did was smoke a little pot. I felt stupid as Adam looked at me. My foolishness mingled with anger too—at myself for not understanding what was going on right in front of me, and at her for not telling me, for making me feel like our rift was my fault.

I remembered a trip Sarah and I had taken to Bakersfield a few weeks earlier. We sat in her friend's truck behind some shabby apartment buildings for a long time, waiting for someone to meet us. Drowsy from the heat and sleep deprived, I didn't give a second thought to the package we brought back, hidden under the passenger seat. *It's just pot, nothing serious*, I thought. I was too sleepy to worry that we were driving into a national park, where even the smallest infraction is a federal offense.

The worry I hadn't felt those few weeks ago suddenly surfaced, like a hard and stinging slap. Nothing in my experience had prepared me for something like this.

My awareness of how entwined I am with the party life here is heightened each time I stay after work in the restaurant to have a glass of wine, or share a bottle of scotch with my brother, Christopher, who has worked in the park as long as I have. Its evidence is omnipresent, visible in more than just photographs. I work with people who have returned to this same park every season for fifteen years or longer. And almost every night, like a ritual, they sit at the bar and drink, telling the same stories to the bartender, forgetting they've told them before. They talk about the peaks they've climbed, with a glass of liquor in one hand and a hand-rolled cigarette in the other. In a place other than Sequoia, we'd call them drunks or think that there's something wrong with them. Here, they're our friends.

I watch the new employees closely, the ones in Sequoia for the first time, many of whom haven't yet learned how to reconcile alcohol and drugs with the solace of this forest. My first season was like this, an exciting summer when I had many close friends and drinking was fun, a way to share our closeness. My roommates and I had parties nearly every night, just like most newcomers to Sequoia, enjoying the first taste of freedom from the constraints of parents, school, and home.

It's difficult to learn how to balance the partying and the wilderness, how not to allow one to eclipse the other. The beauty and isolation of wilderness allows many people to engage or to commune with the natural world. In drinking we can also engage, in a different sort of communion. Both provide the same intoxicating effects. In Sequoia, though, drinking and drugs seem to separate us from the landscape and from one another, rather than drawing us closer. It's as if our desire to engage with the natural world has been misplaced, and drinking is an easier path than climbing a tall mountain peak.

Now, in my last season, I try to understand how much drinking has to do with all the places here that remain unvisited. When did we become lazy or apathetic and lose that balance? When did these pastimes overshadow the reasons we first came here? I keep thinking about how much Keith resembles me, all those seasons ago.

My third season.

I slowly dragged the clean, damp towel along the imitation-wood counter of the bar for the third time while I waited for the last few tables to leave. I took the bar towel to the hostess stand and started to wipe the menus, sticky with thick steak sauce and sweet mango relish.

The glass front doors to the restaurant slammed open. *Probably more Europeans,* I thought. They always seem to arrive just as we are closing.

Without even looking up I said, "Sorry. We closed at nine."

"No, no, you gotta help us." The words were breathless, slurred.

I put down the menu in my hands, annoyed. Two young guys stood there, out of breath as if they had run all the way. They were both employees. One clutched his chest, bent.

"Accident, there's been an accident, we need to call the rangers." He smelled strongly of beer, and was having a hard time getting the words out. The urgency in his voice, despite the numbing effects of alcohol, was unmistakable.

"Here." I pushed the telephone at him. "Just dial 9-1-1, the dispatcher will connect you." He yanked the receiver off the hook and dialed, his hands trembling.

The other young man had regained his breath, and stood up. He looked at me through narrow, watery eyes, as if he might cry.

"What happened?"

He didn't say anything for a second. "Jeremy, he fell, he fell off Moro Rock."

Jeremy had served me breakfast and lunch in the cafeteria nearly every day during the past month. He was shy. He had a crooked, naive smile. And he was only nineteen years old.

He took a deep breath. "We were up there hanging out, having some beer—he just fell over the side." His friend shouted into the phone, almost unintelligibly.

The horrifying image flashed through me. Moro Rock is a huge boulder 1,500 feet tall—one of Giant Forest's most popular places. Tourists wait patiently to climb, single-file, the concrete staircase that winds around and around the grayish-white granite. At the top, they see a panoramic view of the entire San Joaquin Valley. I thought about the metal railing that surrounded the top of Moro Rock. The only things over the edge were more jagged granite cliff faces—and then several thousand feet of nothing to the foothills below.

He spoke to me again. "I tried to catch him, you know?"

His body started to shake, slowly. "I tried to grab his foot as he started to fall . . . " He turned away. His friend hung up the phone and began shouting again, rapid, confusing words I couldn't put together. Other restaurant employees rushed over. I stood there in a jumble of voices and questions I didn't understand. I had gone to Moro Rock with a bunch of friends and countless bottles of wine more times than I could remember. I'd climbed over the railing and leaned back in a weather-carved indentation in the rock, dangled my feet over the edge as we laughed and talked, and kept drinking.

The day before, I'd waited in line for a long time to use the pay phones. Jeremy had stood next to me, silently kicking rocks on the dusty ground. When it was his turn, he shrugged his shoulders and said, embarrassed, "Have to call the parents—you know how they are . . . "

It was already very dark in the forest. Even if he were still alive, the rangers would never find him before morning. No one would even get a chance to say goodbye.

After five summers I've become used to this once-new landscape and its people. When I first arrived at Sequoia, I noticed everything. I spent hours watching ground squirrels and black bears, hiking through granite cliffs in the backcountry, trying to take in my surroundings all at once. The dramatic size of the Western landscape is humbling, and allowed me to put my own life, my burdens, into perspective, in a way the Midwest never could.

Eventually, though, I fell into a comfortable pattern, following the same routine day after day. In many ways, each season in Sequoia resembles the life I so desperately fled back in Indiana, when I wanted to shed the flatness, the monochromatic landscape of a small town, and the sameness of the people there. Perhaps it is exactly that sense of familiarity here that has led to my acceptance of the physical landscape, and the drinking and drugs that are part of it for me. Or perhaps this is why so many of us have become complacent. We've become so intimate with the Sequoia landscape that it is, in a sense, boring. It's easier to rely on the feelings alcohol and drugs evoke than it is to recapture that sense of wonder we all felt at the beginning. We keep searching for the intoxication that the forest itself once brought.

I raise my head to look at the shadows of people and buildings. The cracked concrete digs into my skin through my clothing, and I'm cold. It seems inappropriate, but I'd really like a glass of wine right now, something to warm my body. The crowd has thinned; fragments of conversation fade as people disappear into the forest darkness—laughter, stories, words that no longer have anything to do with this exact moment. We just pretend to forget so quickly here, thankful that it wasn't us. That it happened to someone else, this time. I know without thinking that the others will go back to their cabins, continue sharing stories as they pass around a bottle of something. But we can't really forget. The memories will always linger.

Those who do remain in the parking lot are first-season employees, still watching, listening, standing by themselves. In this still summer night, we're all trying to make sense of what's happened. I may never understand my friend Keith's longing, the burdens he carries in the forest, or those of the countless people who've passed through my life here. My only understanding is that they are part of us all, holding fast with each season that passes, surfacing to remind us of what we each carry.

I start walking again, and my arm brushes against a young man, still almost a boy. He can't be older than eighteen or nineteen. He looks down at the ground, the smooth skin of his forehead twisted in confused worry. I walk past him, thinking about reaching out, touching him on the shoulder. He glances up at me and I smile, hoping that this gesture alone is reassuring.

Halfway up the small hill next to the hotel, my eyes follow the road that will guide me home in the darkness. I reach for the straps of my backpack and shift my weight. With a slight pull, the heavy bottle falls backward. My backpack is half-open, and the sound of breaking glass startles me. In that instant, the sound scares and surprises me, then the emotion blurs into annoyance. For two years I've carefully and deliberately saved this bottle of wine, preserved it through everything. On the ground, splinters of green glass shimmer in the faint yellow glow of the streetlights and a dark red stream trickles down the road.

When I look closely, the glass reminds me of bright sunlight through sugar pine trees. Relieved of the weight, all I can do is laugh. My laughter echoes loudly in the night, a clear voice rising above the sounds between the cabins. I bend down to pick up the large pieces and turn back to the road.

Pretty Enough

Janet Smith

I

I am in the backseat of my parents' Dodge Swinger, my dad taking the curves slowly up the two-lane highway that dead-ends in Yosemite Valley. My sister sits snugged to the door on her side of the backseat. We have been sitting in the car, the backs of our thighs sticking to the vinyl upholstery, since leaving LA seven hours ago. We passed the wooden sign announcing, *Entering Yosemite National Park.* We are waiting. Finally, we enter Wawona Tunnel. When we emerge, blinking in the sun, the valley stands before us, more beautiful than the backdrop of a Disney movie. I begin to cry. My parents get quiet, possibly annoyed.

I feel embarrassed, but at the same time something clenches inside me. A stake is placed. I am awkwardly changed and new. I have to go on in my clammy girlish existence, but inside, something irrevocable has taken hold.

At twelve, I fell in love with Yosemite the way other girls in the 1970s fell in love with Bobby Sherman or David Cassidy. And like a woman I knew who "Elvis-ized" her home—his sweaty likeness on her coffee cup, calendar, and clock—I made a fetish of Yosemite. Under the lunch pavilion at school, I hunched over a library book of glossy photographs of Yosemite. I pored over those pictures the way teenaged boys pore over centerfolds of large-breasted naked women.

I had a typical trifecta of adolescent ailments: crooked teeth with an overbite, a receding chin, and a permanent rash of acne spread across my face, neck, chest, and back. I was also five feet ten at a time when I couldn't appreciate any benefits regarding my Amazonian proportions. The casual persecutions of the boys at Oak Avenue Junior High taught me that I was ugly. I believed it, and that belief bloomed in me and writhed like a parasitic vine around my sense of self. When I hiked in Yosemite, however, I didn't need to worry about how I looked. No one looked at me, and that in itself was a relief. Yosemite was a refuge from and a shield against my grating sense of inadequacy. I wasn't attractive like I was supposed to be, so I attached myself to a place that I and everyone else agreed was monumentally beautiful. Literally, I thought the beauty of Yosemite would rub off on me.

I stared at photos of Yosemite to gather up a feeling. The clean, shining granite, the stark and changeable light, the dim entrances to pine forests all promised a sort of happiness to be had by walking and looking. I constructed a canopy of meaning from this, a sturdy mood to shelter myself. Loving Yosemite would prevent me from blundering into the life I feared awaited me. What exactly did I fear? That I'd end up like the girls and women I saw around me, pushing baby strollers or shopping for another pair of shoes at the mall, or driving to work on the freeway, chewing gum, checking their makeup in the rear-view mirror. I dreaded having what I thought of as an "average life," living according to the advice offered in *Cosmo* and *Glamour:* Be pretty and sexy, catch a man, have a child, buy a house, get a job.

Yosemite took the place of a lover. Yosemite was my private cult, worshipped mostly from afar through the photos of Sierra Club books and calendars. No one I knew in LA felt that way.

At thirteen, I found a book in the library titled *Ranger in*

Skirts. Copyrighted twenty years earlier, it told the story of a young woman fresh from college who spends the summer working as a ranger in Yosemite. She faces a few predicaments, but by the conclusion, she not only has begun an outdoorsy career, she gets a ranger boyfriend as well. I wanted to be like her.

That meant I needed to get good grades in school, especially in biology and the other -ologies. My problem was the processes of osmosis and photosynthesis simply floated out of my brain. I just couldn't believe in them even though my future as a ranger in Yosemite depended on my going to college and majoring in some brand of science.

When I failed my final exam in biology, I cast off my dream of being a ranger. To get to Yosemite, I would need another plan.

II

In 1975, the week after I turned eighteen, my mom dropped me off on the steps of Yosemite Lodge in a snowstorm. A half-hour later I returned with a key to a shared dorm room, a voucher for dinner in the lodge cafeteria, and a slip of paper that stated I had signed a seasonal contract to work as a maid—roomskeeper they called it—for Yosemite Park & Curry Company.

My mother had decided to save the money on a motel room and drive back to LA that night. I waited impatiently for the good-byes to be over, hoping no one would hear her last-minute warnings, that no one would see the hug I returned with stiff arms. That no one would see her brushing snow from my hair.

My mother usually showed her affection by nagging. Always, she ended conversations with a commanding "Don't pick!" referring to my face. When I was nervous, I'd squeeze any festering pimples.

"You'll scar," she warned.

I pulled my canvas Girl Scout backpack out of the trunk and hoisted it on one shoulder. I felt my freedom like a loyal presence. Chugging through snowdrifts to my room, everything I owned I now carried in a backpack, including a book Dad had given me as a going-away present: *How I Found Freedom in an Unfree World.*

I knocked on a door marked K-12 before using my key, but it was unlocked. No one was inside. The room contained a set of bunk beds, a banged-up dresser, and a mirror that had once been part of an elegant vanity. Tacked to the closet, a poster of Lee Majors, shirt unbuttoned and thumbs hooked around his belt buckle, leered at me from across the room. Towels hung from the curtain rods; shoes and underwear and magazines scattered the floor. Pot and incense hung heavy and sweet in the air. Cigarettes, lipsticks, hand creams, and beer bottles littered the dresser top. A dying spider plant hung from an elaborate macramé contrivance.

Home.

"I was sick with worry," my mother later told me. "About you."

"You never said a thing."

"No," she agreed. "It wouldn't have done any good."

She was right, of course. I believed in destiny. I believed Yosemite was mine.

It snowed that February afternoon like all the snowstorms we remember, which are always wilder and more violent than current versions. The limbs of oaks broke under the weight of the heavy, wet snow called "Sierra cement"; the granite monoliths of the valley were bright with fresh snow plastered to every ledge and nook. Tourists latched on tire chains and bumped and clattered down the road.

I could stay now. As long as I liked. That first day, in fact, I decided that I would never leave.

I had no college education, no job skills, no obvious talents, nor any prettiness so essential toward making a young woman's life conventionally unfold. Living in Yosemite was now the visible testament that I wasn't like the rest of the girls I'd grown up with, worrying about split ends and if their boyfriends were just using them for sex. The four-story-high Jeffrey and lodgepole pines were the right size when I passed under their branches. I didn't worry that I wouldn't fit in. For this place, I was the right size.

Yosemite gave me a job and three meals a day deducted from my bimonthly paycheck. It gave me a life as clean as a bone.

In the park, the standards for appearance were not as high as in LA. Girls went without makeup and didn't curl their hair. They wore long skirts with hiking boots. I stopped shaving my legs. I stopped wearing a bra. I began to walk big. I swung my arms; I let my feet fall with a clomp. For the first time in my life, I let myself take up some room. I paid attention to the sky. I let the sun beat down on my head, and I squinted, open-mouthed, if I saw anything interesting. I had no business, no program, and no particular reason to be someplace. I dawdled everywhere.

My new home, K Dorm, was one of four bungalows that formed the lodge's employee quarters along with a scattering of cabins and a huddle of Army-style canvas tents on wooden platforms called the O-Zone. Almost everyone who lived here was under twenty-five and spent their nights looking for sex, drugs, and booze, or all of the above. The partying and the sight of men—bare-chested, hair tousled from sleep—walking out of other girls' rooms in the morning distracted me. I, however, had my copy of *The Natural History of the Sierra Nevada* on the shelf to remind me that I wasn't in Yosemite to wrestle on a cot all night with a nineteen-year-old guy looking to get laid. Anyway, I had not a morsel of confidence in myself as a young woman. The zits, the weak chin, the overbite. I weighed myself up on the sex appeal scale: It tipped the wrong way. Competing with the other girls for male attention was a losing game; the only way I knew how to feel whole was to retreat into the forest.

Half a mile away, managers and full-time National Park Service employees lived in charming stone and wood cottages with lawns and garages. The houses looked entrenched; they were built to be part of the scenery. One row of executive houses faced Stoneman Meadow and a spectacular view of Half Dome. A walking path passed in front of the houses between the wild meadow on one side and the residents' well-tended flowerbeds and clipped lawns on the other. The executives got a view, and the dorms faced a parking lot. They had fences and backyards.

We lived our lives in public.

III

I learned how to be a maid. We were expected to clean a minimum of twelve rooms per shift. We stalled over the last rooms in order not to be assigned to help some lazy or hungover fellow maid who'd fallen behind. The guests—eager, tired, cameras slung round their necks—waited in the lobby while we worked.

We wore our work-issued, checked shirts with ragged jeans and mismatched gloves. When the weather warmed we switched to tight cut-offs, flip-flops, scruffy huaraches. We worked in teams of two. Seasoned maids showed me how to water the liquor, so guests would never know it had been touched, and how to sneak potato chips or cookies without arousing suspicion that they'd been munched. One day, a little girl and her father walked in on me with my hand in her Easter basket. Some maids sampled the makeup and cologne left on the bathroom sink as casually as if it were a department store counter. One of the maids shaved with a guest's razor. And once—even now I blush to write this—I sprayed slept-on sheets with room freshener so I wouldn't have to strip the bed. Fortunately, the guests complained and I was sent back to change the sheets.

No one wanted to clean the cabins because of the snow. You had to trundle through the slush or drifts, pushing a large, square cart on bicycle wheels, loaded with broom, mop, buckets, soap, and clean linen. Squirrels ran across the fresh sheets piled in the carts, leaving spidery tracks. When it snowed, we covered everything on the cart with flapping plastic garbage bags—and still it got wet. I wore my new hiking boots that leaked through their Vibram soles. Each night, in my room, I set the boots next to the heater vent; by June the toes had curled up like elf shoes.

The work wasn't easy, but I didn't feel entitled to a cushier job. When the company decided we needed to present a more professional image and foisted orange-and-brown uniforms on us, I complained about how the cheap polyester made me sweat rather than the enforced meal plan or the low pay. I didn't think I deserved better work conditions. Besides, complaints fell on deaf ears. Curry Co. operated on the idea that working in Yosemite was compensation for the cramped housing and the crummy cafeteria meals.

"Look where you live," a manager might say to rebut an employee complaint.

So, living—literally—in the shadow of Half Dome equated to a better life. And everything from the matches we folded upright in the ashtrays to the pockets of our uniform shirts bore a simplified Half Dome insignia. Even now, it's ubiquitous. We were part of that system: the Half Dome symbol's people.

And I did feel lucky.

IV

In spite of my haphazard work ethic, I was promoted to short-order cook, frying chickens and defrosting pizzas at the fast food café in Yosemite Village. It wasn't hard work, just greasy. All I had to do to make the pizzas was dribble sauce and cheese on Frisbee-like discs of dough and slide them in the oven.

Cal, the night cook, was a tall, skinny guy who wore high-fashion platform shoes, even at work. A pink plastic comb stuck at a jaunty angle into his Afro. He wore sunglasses indoors. He was often stoned. If we didn't play it too loud, we were allowed to have a cassette player in the kitchen. Cal loved disco. He'd bob his head to the beat as he dumped a box of pre-battered drumsticks into the oil drum–sized deep fryer. The beat bounced off the bare white walls. Fried chicken grease puddled the floor. Cal's two-tone platform shoes slid across the linoleum. The pink comb danced on his hair.

Tourists want to see rangers, however, not maids, not fry cooks. Rangers are like Mounties: a quaint, photogenic version of law enforcement. From a tourist's point of view, they are small-town sheriffs, dispensing information while keeping a watchful eye out for shenanigans. Some of them ride horses. They wear cool hats.

But the rest of us who worked at the lower-end jobs? Park Service, the upper echelon of Curry Co., and the tourists crammed onto tour buses with eight hours to sightsee the valley would have preferred for us to magically disappear as soon as our shifts were done. The eighteen-year-olds who bussed tables in the cafeteria looked like the hoodlums back in the city—the ones vacationers hoped to leave behind.

Yosemite seems to operate best as a place apart, untouched by social strife. Those workers in polyester with Half Dome embroidered on their chests spoil Yosemite as free-floating scenic refuge. They drag in the workaday world of haves and have-nots, of labor and its discontents.

I was one of the employees sunbathing topless in the meadow. Or listening to heavy metal music. Or draping ugly laundry out of a dorm window to dry. When your only private space is the approximate size of a prison cell, sitting on a porch or on the hood of a car in a parking lot makes sense.

The dorms' taupe paint and bunker-esque design were meant to blend into the surroundings. But it was harder to blend us in. We were workers, and the sight of workers, especially low-paid ones, clashed with the photogenic vistas. The valley was glossy granite, cascading water—we were junky cars, the smell of pot.

If you are taught as a child that you will grow up to perform manual labor and that most work is both tiresome and tiring, it is no great hardship to work at menial jobs. In Yosemite, on and off over the next twenty years, I worked as a maid, short-order cook, table busser, and waitress. I guarded the Ahwanee Hotel at night when a disgruntled ex-employee-turned-arsonist set fires at the warehouse and the Curry Village skating rink.

I saved up for braces, had my overbite and receding chin corrected, and gratefully swallowed Accutane tablets that finally and permanently cured my acne. At thirty-two, I was offered a job as a cocktail waitress at the Mountain Room Bar. Nobody admitted it, but it was expected that only attractive girls were hired as cocktail waitresses. Yes, I would make good tips, but the real promotion was that the management thought I was pretty.

The entire object in being a cocktail waitress is to get tips. I noticed immediately that the cutest girl with the largest chest made the most money. She swayed about on high-heeled, lace-up ankle boots as though she'd been born in them. She cinched her uniform vest with a large safety pin in back to pull it tight in front; it seemed her breasts were ready to bust through her shirt.

The other girls at the bar tried to help me. They suggested hairstyles, gave me makeup tips, and warned me about guys who'd try to run a hand up your skirt while ordering a drink. They showed me how to puff my shirt out at the opening of my vest to present the illusion of a bosom.

I had reached the apex of my Yosemite career. I had a well-paid job. Now and then a man would tell me I was pretty.

And somehow it wasn't enough.

V

I decided to leave. I remember feeling driven. I remember feeling like I could leave and not walk around like half of me was in permanent shadow. I had come to Yosemite for beauty I did not possess, but the years I spent among the granite had transformed me. Once I no longer needed to lose myself in the wilderness, I no longer needed the park. I abandoned Yosemite with the same single-mindedness with which I'd claimed it.

One bright, late October day, I drove past Bridalveil Falls and looked in my rear-view mirror for that last glimpse of the valley's walls before the road descends into the canyon. Then I checked my makeup in the mirror. It sounds harsh to write this now, but it's true: I was finally pretty enough for the rest of the world.

Grizzly Country

Joseph Flannery

We are not supposed to be here. Dave stays behind the wheel of the Jeep, and I step out to unlock the gate. Next to the blockade, a sign warns employees:

"DANGER. GRIZZLY BEARS FREQUENT THIS AREA. ABSOLUTELY NO FOOT TRAVEL BEYOND THIS POINT."

"Are you sure this is okay?" Dave asks when I climb back in. The area is strictly off-limits—even to us employees—unless we're completing official work.

I glance into the side-view mirror. No one around.

"Yeah, let's go."

And we drive through.

I am working in Yellowstone National Park for the summer, and I've done so for the past several years, ever since graduation. Coming from California's Central Valley, Yellowstone National Park and the surrounding Northern Rockies feel wild beyond imagination. Moose strip willow branches in the shadows of craggy peaks. Wolves trot along the Lamar River as the sunset turns the cottonwoods to gold. Bison bellow and brawl in the high sage of sweeping valleys during the autumn rut. And of course, the great bear, the grizzly, leaves massive tracks from river bottom to ridge top. His presence, more than any other beast, fills the land.

Past the gate, far out of view of the visitors, our Jeep follows the winding road to a clearing in the pines known as Mesa Pit, which the park staff uses as a carcass dump. In Yellowstone, the National Park Service has an obligation to protect not only the wildlife within the park, but the human visitors as well. So when a large animal—such as a bison or elk—dies in a high-visitor-use area—such as a campground or picnic area—the carcass is removed. If it wasn't, the hundreds of pounds of rotting flesh would attract all sorts of carnivores to scavenge. Including grizzly bears.

Yesterday a thousand-pound bison died outside of a popular geothermal area. Workers in the maintenance division hauled the massive carcass away and dumped it at Mesa Pit.

As part of my job here, I spend a lot of time answering questions and enforcing park rules.

"No, you can't soak in the hot pools," I say. Yet my friends and I know the locations of the very best, and we laugh and soak under winking stars.

"Never, never get too close to a grizzly bear," I warn the visitors. Yet here Dave and I are, driving toward the clearing, the soft muddy dirt quieting our approach.

But we know what we are doing. We live here.

It is early evening. The lodgepole pines crowd the road, blocking out the angled light. The road weaves along the base of a hill, and Dave slows the Jeep to a crawl as the carcass dump comes into view.

The bloated bison sprawls at the center of the clearing, its stiff legs frozen high in the air like in a cartoon. Dave kills the engine. Skulls, horns, ribs, and vertebrae cover the ground. Fur still clings to some.

A coyote pulls at the dead bison. She cowers at our arrival but does not flee, instead eying the Jeep between toothy jerks. Shiny ravens peer down from the dark trees encircling the clearing.

They fidget and flap, impatient spectators awaiting their turn at the flesh. A familiar sweet and nauseating odor fills the Jeep. Flies swarm the truck, bouncing across the windows.

We watch the scene for a moment, disappointed that a bear is not there.

Time to go. Dave reaches toward the ignition. His hand is almost there when the coyote's ears perk, her body swiveling toward the lodgepoles. The ravens cry out and take flight in unison. The coyote slinks away, body low to the ground, tail tucked under. Dave leans forward in his seat, body tense, staring off to the right.

"Something's out there."

I follow his eyes into the darkened wood just beyond our vehicle. A large shadow moves swiftly through the trees. The silhouette is unmistakable, like a cave painting come to life. My skin prickles.

Grizzly.

The great bear bursts into the light. Head held high, he jogs right up to the carcass and swings his front paws down violently, attacking the already dead. The stiff legs jiggle. Within moments, the grizzly opens the bison—his shoulders, head, and neck immediately slick with entrails and blood. At times he rears far into the air and pounds down onto the bison, cracking the ribs. He scoops his front paw deep into the body cavity and pulls out the purple stomach lining.

"Jesus Christ," one of us says. It might have been me.

Most of the really large grizzlies I've seen, the truly frightening ones, are never quite as tall as I thought they'd be. But they are long. Thick and long. It gives them a sleek and sinister look, not cuddly at all, but fast and ferocious. This is the longest grizzly I have ever seen.

The sight of the grizzly flows straight from my eyes down my spinal cord and into my bloodstream. At one point, I realize my body is completely flexed—my head thrust forward, my neck strained. Dave is much the same. His knuckles bulge as he grips the steering wheel. As I watch the bear feed, awestruck, a sudden realization stabs through the haze. I turn to Dave.

"How are we going to leave?"

Dusk creeps into the clearing. It appears the grizzly will be feeding for some time. The narrow, snaking road makes backing out nearly impossible. The only place to turn around passes just by the bear, and our windows are at the same level of his bloody head. I'm afraid of what will happen if Dave starts up the Jeep: the sudden sound of the engine turning over may induce a charge. Grizzlies are unpredictable and aggressive.

Dave reaches toward the ignition. I hold my breath.

I have lived and worked in both grizzly country and bear country, and they are not the same. Bear country, as I define it, is home to *Ursus americanus,* the American black bear. The black bear—sometimes colored brown, cinnamon, or blond—is found in forty-one of the fifty states. If you enjoy the outdoors, chances are you have visited or stayed in bear country. Bear country is where we all camp and ski. Maybe you've seen the toppled trash cans or shredded logs beside the trail; this is evidence of black bear presence. Perhaps you've seen the bears themselves, crossing the road at the edge of your headlights, or meandering through a meadow outside of town.

Grizzly country is different. *Ursus arctos horribilis,* the grizzly bear, roams only five locations in the contiguous United States: in the greater Yellowstone National Park ecosystem, in the Northern Rockies of Montana, and in even smaller slivers of habitat in Idaho and Washington. The grizzly is much larger than its distant relative the black bear, and is easily the most formidable carnivore in North America.

In bear country, when you take your trash out and the

bushes rustle nearby, your heart skips a beat and your pace quickens, but you continue on your way. In grizzly country, the fear starts at the doorway. You peer out into the night, surveying the darkness. You step cautiously down the stairs and freeze, ears cocked, head still. You creep forward and pause again, like a deer crossing into the open. And if the bushes rustle, you drop the trash and sprint into the house.

To understand the way grizzly bears act—and to thus grasp the inherent danger of living alongside them—you must know a little about how they evolved. The grizzly, a subspecies of brown bear, evolved on the desolate tundra of the far north. Resources were scarce. There were no trees for their cubs to climb when pursued by predators. In order to successfully protect food sources and offspring, the grizzly developed an exaggerated aggressiveness. Long ago, the grizzly made the choice between fight or flight. Modern grizzlies, when startled or threatened, charge and attack out of instinctual reflex.

The aggressive disposition of the grizzly has lead to violent encounters, attacks, and even deaths in Yellowstone National Park and the surrounding area. Most of the attacks and encounters are considered avoidable. A photographer had his face peeled off a few summers ago in Hayden Valley, but he survived the attack. Rangers developed his film and discovered the photographer was much too close; the bear was not to blame. A man was killed after he camped illegally in an off-limits area and left copious amounts of food lying around, attracting the grizzly into his campsite. Park officials use this particular death as an example of what can happen as a result of human error.

The vast majority of the bear attacks can be explained by park bear biologists, experts in grizzly behavior: A visitor got too close to a mother and cub. A man hiked alone and failed to make sufficient noise warning bears of his presence. And so on. But there are exceptions.

In the summer of 1984, twenty-five-year-old Brigitta Fredenhagen was ripped from her tent as she slept in the backcountry near Pelican Valley. Park investigators failed to come up with a strong reason for the attack. The young woman's camp was fairly clean; her food hung the required distance from her tent. There were no signs of a struggle. Her body was found 250 yards from her tent. The grizzly was never caught.

In Yellowstone's grizzly country, this story and others are woven into an oral tradition. Live in this land long enough, and soon the accounts are not read in a book or report. They are heard first- or second-hand from people you know and trust. From the friend of the photographer, or the ranger who found the body, or the local rancher who stumbled upon some cubs just outside of the park and heard the mother crashing through the trees toward him.

In his famous essay "Escudilla," Aldo Leopold wrote that, as a young man in grizzly country, "campfire conversation ran to beef, *bailes,* and bear." Leopold worked in the Southwest, which was also cowboy country. "Beef" and *"bailes"* meant talking about work and girls, respectively. Nearly a century later, on a backpacking trip on the edge of the park during my first season, my friends and I covered the same topics around the fire.

We talked about the girls who worked in the park and the girls who lived in town. We complained about work and the park politics, and traded stories from on the job. And of course we talked about grizzlies. One of my companions worked at park headquarters and knew all the best grizzly stories from the longtime employees. We whispered about Brigitta Fredenhagen and how the grizzly stole her away. Our world became a flickering island of yellow light in a sea of inky black. The darkness surrounding our camp shrouded one of the wildest places left in the United States. In the morning we found fresh tracks, larger than my size-12 boot, pressed into the trail just beyond our camp. A large grizzly had passed in the night.

To have a close encounter with a grizzly is to wear a sort of badge of honor around the park. Toward the end of that first season, I remember feeling a little let down that I had not experienced one. I loved the local stories and foolishly wanted one of my own. But it wouldn't be until my second season that I would come across a grizzly, while mountain biking just outside the park.

I had thought it was a rock at first, a large, humped rock rising above the sage in the late-afternoon sun. The rock sat just off the trail, halfway between where I rested and the tree-lined summit ahead. I straddled my bike and studied the rock, catching my breath before the last of the climb. Far below, Wapiti Creek turned out of sight, bending toward its confluence with the Gallatin River, a few miles downstream of the park's northwest boundary. The surrounding country—mighty swells of gray sage, sharp tan rock, and dark-green pine—pushed high into the pale august sky. Absolute grizzly country.

And that rock looked suspect. I cupped my hands to my face and yelled loudly, just to be safe.

"Hey bear!"

The rock moved, and a gigantic head lifted out of the scrub, where it had probably been sniffing for pocket gophers.

Holy shit.

The bear cocked his head like a dog and peered downhill to where I stood. The sun was at my back, and the wind blew across my face. I was almost invisible to him. I froze, no movement, no breath, nothing. A tiny voice whispered instructions from the back of my head, at the base, near my neck.

He can't see you. Flee.

A moment later, the bear's head was down again, shoulders moving. Digging. I lifted the bike between my legs and started an awkward, slow-motion pivot—walking on my tiptoes, clenching my jaw, trying to turn the other way. I was almost all the way around when the grizzly's head snapped back up, ears alert, nose raised in the air.

A moment passed like this—both of us still, except for the flutter of my heart and the flare of his nostrils. And then he was jogging toward me, head raised, neck elongated, eyes scanning. I could tell he still hadn't seen me, that he'd probably just sensed or heard my movement, but he ran to investigate.

I had maybe three or four seconds. The sequence of my thoughts is still quite clear to me today.

First, I thought about a coworker and the mauling he had received the previous fall, leaving him hospitalized. He had been hunting elk, he told us at an employee campfire at park headquarters, and had stumbled upon a mother and cub. The female grizzly pulled him out of the tree he had climbed to escape and pinned him to the ground. At one point, he reached for his rifle and managed to shove it down in her mouth and fire off a round. She didn't stop. The grizzly would die a day later, but the attack continued for an agonizing twenty minutes.

"Bear spray," he had said, referring to the highly concentrated pepper spray sold to hikers and fly fisherman in grizzly country. "That's what I wish I had instead of a rifle that day."

A U.S. Fish and Wildlife report had just been released. The report reviewed grizzly attacks in North America and found that bear spray was effective in stopping an attack 92 percent of the time, as opposed to firearms, which worked only 50 percent of the time.

Remembering this, I reached up and fingered the bear spray can hanging from my shoulder strap—the one that I always carried when biking in high-alpine areas such as this.

The grizzly saw the movement of my arm and zeroed in. His ears flattened, his head sank, his long body stretched out into a powerful stride. Curiosity, it appeared, was suddenly replaced by intent. The little voice piped up again, calling the shots.

Fuck it. Let's go.

What happened next is a blur. I suppose I clipped into my pedals, sucked in as much air as possible, and launched down the trail. I can remember my entire existence became focused on a brightly lit spot at the end of a dark tunnel about four feet in front of my tire. The trail, while bumpy and rock-strewn, was hard-packed and speed-inducing. The wind shrieked past my cheeks, nipping at my ears. A glance over my shoulder would have most definitely generated a crash. I dared not look. I also became dimly aware that I had reached some sort of bike terminal velocity, if there is such a thing, with each pedal stroke failing to increase my speed, despite the proper gear selection.

And again, there was a tiny voice. But it was a different voice this time, and whispered from inside a different cavern of the skull: not from the base, but from somewhere up front.

My god. What a story this is gonna make.

Several miles down the trail, I stopped, aware that the grizzly was no longer in pursuit. I gasped for breath and looked back up the hill, my legs shaking, my energy depleted. The grizzly was nowhere in sight.

I grinned. I had my story.

And I told almost everyone I came across. My boss and my coworkers. The girls who owned the local bike shop. I sent e-mails home about it. I called my parents and nonchalantly worked the story into the conversation, as if it happened every day. Back home, my family and friends all lived in cities or the suburbs. I made it well known that I just happened to live in a place where large predators roamed the countryside. And I liked that.

The bike encounter not only gave me a story, but it also solidified the grizzlies' residence in my little world. They became not just mythical monsters from an old-timer's tale, but real creatures, full of muscle and fright and hot breath. The landscape changed for me. When I biked or hiked, my senses expanded. I scanned the rugged hills and the shadows beneath the pines. I stopped and listened in the willows by the river where I fly-fished. I tilted my nose to the breeze and sniffed like an animal, searching for any presence of the grizzly that still haunted me. To travel alone and unarmed within this land is to feel the electrical current of the wild, to feel a slow drip of adrenaline trickling into your veins.

And I wanted more: another rush, another encounter.

I guess that is why Dave and I are at Mesa Pit, gaping at a blood-covered grizzly through thin glass. We didn't even bring a camera.

Dave's hand pauses by the key, trembling. In a flash, I realize our error.

We should not have come.

Self-loathing and panic rises in my throat. This bear does not see my green and gray uniform; he does not care about the stories, or the campfires, or how much I want the dangers and excitement of a frontier-like life to still exist.

This is how you end up as an example of what not to do in grizzly country. I picture the rangers finding our bodies, shaking their heads and snapping pictures.

"Just be ready to hit that gas," I manage to whisper.

Dave turns the ignition, and the Jeep rumbles to life. The grizzly's head whips up, his black eyes piercing into the cab. Time freezes in the clearing, the great bear silently considering our fate. He returns to the bison, granting us safe passage.

Dave starts slowly back down the road. Toward the small

government trailer I have lived in for only a short time in this ancient world. For I too am a visitor. Only the grizzly has lived here long enough to call this land home.

The Wild Dead

Jeremy Pataky

According to Kelly Bay—the bush pilot who dropped us at the tundra strip—my lone client and I were the first visitors of the season that year at Skolai Pass. It was early June already, and the north-facing slopes in the Wrangell Mountains were still widely blanketed with snow. My client, a photographer, spent an entire day near camp shooting scenics, which he'd come all the way to Wrangell–St. Elias National Park to do. I hiked into Chitistone Pass alone, following the large tracks of a wolf through snow, then mud, then snow again, while a family of plump marmots eyed me from their boulder. The tracks led to a caribou kill, tufts of fur scattered on the snow, a bleached jawbone on yellow lichens and still-brown tundra leaves. Scavengers had carted most of the animal off by then. What bones remained glowed white in the sun, though a patina of red highlighted fissures and cracks on the long comma of the mandible, and blood had pooled and hardened in the gutters between the teeth.

Later, looking down from camp into the broad valley bottom, we watched a herd of seven caribou move with the grace and effortlessness of mist across the braids of Skolai Creek. I saw the animals differently than I would have if I'd not read the story of the wolf's hunt earlier. Beyond the herd, across the valley, on a bench highlighted with a south-facing patch of green, a band of Dall sheep grazed all evening long.

The death I had stumbled upon augmented the life on the land, even a land just beginning its boozy, early yawns and stretches after the long sleep of winter. Watching the caribou trot across the valley, I imagined other, nonhuman eyes regarding them. When I left, animals would continue to watch, stalk, and elude one another in the shifting light, just as they had before I came. My imagination drew a constellation between the caribou remains, the wolf that killed it, and the herd moving a mile away in the valley; the pattern there reminded me that so much was happening that I couldn't see. It is an obvious idea, but not one that is necessarily easy to feel in the gut. Perhaps our faith in otherness, or the desire to feel less estranged from what seems so different from us, is part of the excitement inspired in us when we see wildlife.

A group of white birds, snow buntings, maybe, lifted from the bushes below, flew as one toward the west, then banked with a flash of light off their wings and glided down to settle again. I watched the caribou beyond them and fingered the coarse fur I had stuffed into the pocket of my rain pants back at the kill site.

Most Alaskans share a passion for wild animals. I'm certainly among those who drop what they're doing to watch moose when they step out of the woods into our lives, appearing on trails and roads, in yards and parking lots. I sit and glass the alpine tundra, looking for bears. I study the water for whales and watch for the black eyes, noses, and tail tips of ermine against the snow. Visitors to Alaska invariably hope to encounter, or at least see, wildlife. Over the years, though, I have become equally fascinated not just with Alaska's wildlife, but also with its equally plentiful wild dead.

The remains of dead animals are another type of "sign," like the tracks or scat we are often excited to see and later report to friends. After venturing into the woods and back, I'll mention the steamy pile of berry-filled bear scat that was dropped like pie filling upon the trail sometime during my walk. Or I'll describe the massive ellipsis of grizzly tracks down at the river, perfectly imprinted in the mud, trailing around the bend. Sign is interesting, because it hints at what happens in a place when we aren't around; it permits vicarious witness. Winter snow becomes a canvas that allows us to see who or what came before. We thrill to see the scurried routes of voles, the feather-brushed calligraphy of a ptarmigan or owl in soft powder, the deep postholes left by moose, the round furry footfalls of lynx, the connect-the-dot beelines of snowshoe hares moving bush to bush, our own ski tracks leading back across a frozen lake. All of these traces tell stories about a place. And the presence of dead animals in the landscape contributes to the narrative we glimpse when we see wildlife.

Carcasses and smaller bits of deceased animals litter Alaska's tundra and forests, intertidal and riparian zones, even its glaciers. In August, my clients and I found the delicate bones of a mountain goat a mile out on the Kennicott Glacier—the tapering curve of a single horn, some ribs, a leg bone. Later that evening, we walked between the steep slopes of a mountain and the high wall of the glacier's lateral moraine. About to set up camp after our first day of glacier travel, we came upon a startling scene: an area the size of a bathtub was absolutely red-washed with blood. Scattered on the stain were the bones of another mountain goat. The animal had clearly been torn open here while freshly dead, probably by a bear or wolverine. It was an old site: the blood long since dried, the foul stench wafted away. Farther north we found the remains of yet another goat, apparently killed by an avalanche. The bones, including a skull with horns intact, had melted out of the leftover snow pile along with the wreckage of dried cow parsnip and alder branches, also shorn off the mountain by the slide.

Last year, friends found the remains of two grizzly cubs that had melted out of a late spring avalanche. They noted the location and returned two days later to retrieve them, but all that they found were bone fragments, fur, and bear tracks. A "grisly" scene indeed. It was sunny and warm that week, and glaciers in the valley sweated meltwater into swollen streams. Since hearing that story, I have often imagined a large boar grizzly discovering those snow-preserved cubs just a day or two after the sun wrested them from their burial. What were the sounds of the bear's eating? I've wondered at the strength of those jaws, crunching skulls the way I might bite into hard candy.

Another bush pilot once described to me the patterns in the snow made by wolverines after finding a winter kill. A wolverine will remove a piece of a carcass and walk away in a straight line, caching the morsel for a future meal. Then it returns, takes more, and walks away again at a slightly different heading. A wolverine will repeat this until the entire carcass is safely stashed, unwittingly drawing a picture that is there to be read by the few people who happen to fly over the radiating wagon wheel of tracks.

What story is told in the sloppy mess of our own boot prints, strewn between parking lots and the gaping doors of supermarkets in town?

One of my first Alaska backpacking trips occurred in Denali National Park. It rained the entire time. A few miles in, we set up a base camp and then hiked neighboring valleys and ridges. Near the banks of a stream, amid a tangle of alder and willow, we came across a massive, well-palmated moose antler that appeared to have been shed long ago. Looking closely, I saw the chiselings of rodents that had gnawed the bone for its calcium.

Moss had started to grow on the antlers, hastening their decomposition. We marveled at the ecological thrift manifested in that chewed bone, the idea that a significant part of a moose could be consumed as nourishment by other creatures and plants before the moose even died.

I suppose that the Denali moose whose antler I found is dead by now. A few years have passed since I found it. And judging by the antler's size, its owner had been a mature bull. Did the moose die of old age? Was it taken down by a wolf pack? Did it wander out of the park and get shot? Is it a trophy mounted in some Midwesterner's den, its glass eyes reflecting television, dinner parties, the family dog? Did its flesh become the flesh of wolves, ravens, eagles, magpies, foxes, beetles, bears? Did some shifting braid of a glacial river slowly submerge the leaky hull of its pelvis? Is it possible that no person ever saw the bull while it lived? And how has my experience of the world been affected by the discovery of that half-rotten, rain-soaked antler beside a minor, unnamed creek, shed by an anonymous old moose, once vibrantly alive and now dead?

Coffee in hand, I look out a window from the top level of the house, down toward stubborn daisies and dying yarrow that have grown up around the garden. Many moose have been visiting the yard lately. None in sight today, though I know that if I went out and walked into the wet grass, I would find their cleft prints, the little brown dirigibles of their scat, some birch branches stripped of leaves.

I imagine a diptych of two images: teeth marks where a moose stripped bark from an aspen trunk beside the small trails gnawed by a porcupine into an antler. I'm learning to see these tracings, to watch for sign, to feel awe before a world always becoming itself, a story ever unfolding.

The Weight of a Harlequin

Mary Beth Baptiste

STRETCH. PULL. WRENCH.

My shoulder joints threaten to split apart as Tim and I churn the canoe through the white-crested waves of Jackson Lake. Water fans over the bow, soaking my raingear. To the south, gravid clouds obscure Grand Teton National Park's signature peaks. Gusts whip at us, thrusting us northward and filling our lungs with a scent of crystalline blue–brown. Paddling in a solo canoe 30 meters away, our coworker Julian cants his ruffled forehead into the wind and charges ahead like a gladiator.

Tim, my supervisor, has asked me to help out on a two-day harlequin duck survey in Webb Canyon. He studied these elusive ducks for his master's research and continues the project as part of his job at the park. Classified as "sea ducks," *Histrionicus histrionicus* live in clear, fast-moving mountain creeks where they feast on stoneflies, caddisflies, and mayflies. The drakes mate in the Northern Rockies in the spring, then take off to spend summers in coastal areas of the Pacific Northwest. Their mates stay behind to lay and incubate the eggs and raise the young to fledging. Now, in early August, we'll look for broods of females and young, capture them in nets, take measurements, and band them.

My excitement threatens to float me away. Working with wildlife in a primo Rocky Mountain park has been a lifelong dream. Finally, at forty, I'm putting to work my ancient master's degree in wildlife biology as a biotech in Grand Teton's Science & Resource Management Division. By default, I'm twenty years older than the average National Park Service seasonal employee. But I soothe my wilted ego by reminding myself that the silver strands coursing through my chocolate-brown ponytail are few and barely noticeable.

Progress across the lake is slow. With every stroke, I lean ahead and draw the paddle hard through the water, twisting my spine to its limit, throwing all my strength into the motion. As my shoulders go giddy-numb, my muscles tingle with the work. I relish every stretch. Finally I'm using my whole body, living my whole life, shooting it all.

This is new for me. Back in Massachusetts, where I came from, I tiptoed through life in fussy clothes and impractical shoes. Like everyone I knew, I lived life with much to spare. I held back, saved it for storms. This was the approach to life I'd been raised with: "It's too hot to ride your bike to the library," my mother would say, setting her soft chin primly over her eyelet collar. "It would tax your heart." My grandmother would nod in agreement as she reached into her pocketbook for the keys to her sky-blue Ford.

But here, restraint is an alien concept. No task is off-limits. That my coworkers fearlessly scurry over alpine terrain to search for bighorn sheep and rappel off cliffs to band birds fills me with awe.

"*MB*." Tim's voice slashes through the wind as I feel a gritty thrust under the canoe. "Snag off to port. Pull. *Hard.*"

A sickening grind, a lurch. Less than a hand's length from the gunwales, tree branches poke out from the water like desperate arms. I extend over the starboard side, jam the paddle into the water, and draw, pulling the boat with me. The canoe rocks side to side like a Weeble before leveling. Branches rake the bottom of the boat, no doubt leaving jagged scratches in the green fiberglass.

When I turn around, Tim's staring pop-eyed from under grizzled eyebrows. "Hew-*eee*," he says. We'd come close to flipping the canoe and dumping pricey optics and gear, along with ourselves, in the drink.

The water level in Jackson Lake varies with Idaho potato farmers' irrigation demands. This week, the water is high, and rooted trees lurk just below the surface.

"Must have rained in Idaho last week," I say, dipping my paddle.

Cloud remnants banner around Elk Ridge and thin into fog along its slopes. Upcanyon, rock ridges undulate skyward. Dark spruces and firs litter the slopes like iron filings.

As we approach the west lakeshore, the wind fizzles, and straw-colored light overlays the landscape. Funneling the canoes through an opening in the willows, we course through a vegetation-choked passageway to a clearing. I jump out and pull our canoe onto the shore.

"Let's drop off the heavy stuff at the cabin," Tim says.

I laugh at the ruckus that follows. At six foot four, and with the strength and stamina of a locomotive, Tim feels a 30-pound daypack as little more than a ripple in his pocket. He effortlessly straps on his footlocker-sized pack, hooks a dry bag of food and a spotting scope onto his elbow, and reaches back into the canoe.

Arching his gnarly eyebrows, Julian hoists on his own coffin-sized pack, then jostles Tim aside to snatch up the sack of bird-banding gear first. "I'll get that," he says.

Their muscling and grunting as they load up reminds me of chest-thumping behavior in other primates. Do they realize how they unconsciously spar with one another, trying to establish alpha dominance? I find myself, though, succumbing to the thrill of the task and jumping into the fray with them. This is the wildlife biology I've always longed to do; I mustn't allow any scent of HEF (helpless eastern female) to leak out. Strapping my sopping raingear to my breadbox-sized pack, I heave the thing onto my back, trying to appear tough and confident. With waders slung over my arm, I lift the Playmate cooler from the canoe.

Dewy willows ribbon over my arms and torso as I plod through them, holding the cooler above my head. It weighs heavy on my wrists; I suspect it contains Tim's home brew and some kind of game meat. I shout my bear deterrent: "*Hey* bears, we're coming through . . ." The guys, with jutting chins and stomping feet, trudge along silently.

At the far end of a jade-colored meadow, the shuttered Lower Berry patrol cabin comes into view. It is, I decide, a perfect little log cabin in the woods—a cozy interface between wild nature and civilization, but on a humble scale; a morsel of civilization in a sea of nature, a welcome reversal to modern society's lopsidedness.

The narrow porch is cluttered with stacked firewood and a plywood, pointy-roofed enclosure that holds emergency and firefighting equipment. A litter is suspended by bungee cords from the roof overhang.

Tim unlocks the door to the smell of dry wood. Inside is a jumble of cupboards, a woodstove, a propane camp stove, a dinged-up table with two chairs, and bunks with bare mattresses. Gear dangles from the roof joists. From our pile of supplies, we sort out what we'll need for the day. We claim bunks with our sleeping bags, stash food on the shelves. It's a luxury to have a place to secure our food while we're out—we're spared having to rope it up in a tree to protect it from bears.

After a trip to the outhouse, I sit on the cabin porch and watch clouds evaporate from the sky. Breezes whisper through trees. The creek gurgles. A red-tailed hawk soars toward Harem Hill, crying *screent*. A warbler chortles from the willows. Until I'd experienced full silence broken only by wild sounds, I hadn't realized how much I'd missed it. I think of John Muir, who diverted Yosemite Creek to run beneath the floor of the cedar and pine cabin he built. Plants grew through the floorboards and frogs chirped beneath him while he slept. Realizing that wild sounds will lull me to sleep tonight comforts me.

Webb Canyon is one of Grand Teton's remote northern canyons. It lies along the shores of Moose Creek, beneath stony peaks named for charismatic megafauna: Elk Mountain, Owl Peak, Moose Mountain. The northern canyons are where the grizzlies are, and the specter of confronting one is never far from my consciousness. While I wait for Tim and Julian, I rummage through the top compartment of my pack for my foolproof bear repellent: a handful of pebbles in a small V8 juice can, the opening covered with a square of duct tape. According to the experts, a metallic clanking noise deters bears, because it's a sound that doesn't occur naturally in the wild.

To get into the canyon, we canoe across the outlet of Moose Creek and lash the boats to willows on its gravelly shore. The harlequin duck habitat begins three miles upcanyon, so we have about an hour's hike before we need to boot up in our waders. Mine, lashed across the top of my pack, swing and slap my shoulders with every step, but I ignore them.

The guys bolt ahead of me. Even though we're all at comparable levels of fitness, I could never keep up with their long-legged strides. I've never been in Webb Canyon, don't know where I'm going. There's nothing I can do but settle into my own pace and hope they wait for me at any trail intersections.

The sky has rinsed clear and now screams in classic Western garish blue, with a few benign cloud rivulets to the west. Right now my world consists of sun, sky, trees, flowers, earth, rocks.

Pivoting around, I make a mental list of my surroundings: cluster of subalpine fir to the north; willow-fringed shoreline to the south, with a few aspens, Douglas firs, and lodgepole pines jutting through. In the meadows: yellow mule's ears, purple larkspur, crimson Indian paintbrush, peach-colored buckwheat, bubbly rocks coated with green and orange lichens, patches of huckleberry bushes drooping with ripe berries that I pick and pop into my mouth as I pass. No animal tracks yet. As I enter a dense purpose of fir and pine, a sandhill crane croaks overhead. Looking up, I spot a scrap of wing through the knitted boughs. The trail meanders ahead, blurry with dust, calling me into the wilderness that I now call home.

With one thumb hooked in my pack's shoulder strap, I get into a walking rhythm that matches my heartbeat. A song my grandmother sings plays in my mind, "In the Blue Ridge Mountains of Virginia, on the Trail of the Lonesome Pine . . ." It rolls on and on, ending only to turn back on itself and rerun in a slightly different key, a musical Möbius strip.

But while I love the scrabble of color, the blaze of sun, the cacophony of woodsy sounds and smells, I'm aware that the guys are out of view, out of earshot. I'm doing something we always advise against in the park literature that we ourselves write: I'm hiking alone in grizzly country. Only a V8 can and a few stones stand between me and the silvertips. I pick up the pace, rattle the can more vigorously, and yell, "Comin' through, bears! Outta the way!"

Moose Creek cascades over logjams spewing spray and tan foam. Finally, where the salmon-colored pinnacles rise up near the rocky cliffs of Elk Mountain and Owl Peak, I'm relieved to spot the guys ahead in a clearing. Tim lies on his back with binoculars glued to his eyes; Julian hunkers down to peer through a spotting scope. They're scanning the peaks for bighorn sheep and peregrine falcons.

"Hey." I worm out of my pack and fish out my water bottle. No answer.

"See anything?" I ask.

"Nope." Tim's eyes never unlock from his binoculars.

When I peel off my NPS ball cap, my bangs are pasted to my forehead in slimy strings. I sprawl on my back in the grass, draw out my own binocs, and rest my head on my pack. Soft nubbles of grass, cones, and pebbles press through my gray uniform shirt, warming my back, their heat intensified by this throbbing, high-altitude sunlight.

After glassing the peaks for a while, we continue up the canyon until a finger of willows curls toward the trail. Tim stops, pulls off his sunglasses, and paws sweat off the bridge of his nose. "The creek starts braiding here," he says. "We can each take a section." When, without warning, he strips down to his BVDs to pull on his chest waders, my eyelids peel up as I turn away.

The rubber of my waders burns hot as I pull them up over my green uniform jeans. But when I wade into a deep pool, the heat dissipates, and a cool compression massages my legs from ankle to thigh like rubber antiembolism stockings. I head to one of the channels of the creek, where the water slows and broadens.

My willow-choked strand of creek curves to the south and then west. Sloshing through it is slow. I focus on every step, balancing on rounded cobbles. Every few steps I glass the water up- and downstream, paying particular attention to streamside rocks and their shadowy overhangs. But all I see are water striders that look as big as grape leaves through the binoculars.

Eventually we all meet up on a gravel bar.

"Any luck?" I ask.

"Nope," Julian says, combing his long fingers through his beard.

Tim swats at a gnat on his arm. "*Nada*. Let's head upstream."

We continue on, a raggedy wader parade, to a fragrant stand of subalpine fir.

"Let's split up again. Julian, you stay here. Hide in those willows there. I'll head about half a mile upstream. MB, you scan in between. Stay low. If you see any ducks, herd them downstream toward Julian." Tim ambles on up the trail, dust clinging to his waders.

I act like I know what I'm doing. I follow Tim and make mental calculations: If he's going a half-mile, how far is that on the ground? How much time? About ten minutes? Maybe less for the stilt-man. To be on the safe side, I check my watch and go off trail after about six minutes. I wriggle through the willows to the creek bank. Poking around, I find a mica-speckled rock hidden in the shrubbery where I can sit straight-legged while scanning the creek through an opening in the branches. After a few crackers and a bite of cheese, I get comfortable for the survey.

Botanists have it easy, I think, fingering a leaf of *Salix,* willow. Wildlife biology can be tedious, lonely work: long hours of sitting still and waiting for animals to come to us. Peering through binoculars with my elbows levitating at my sides, my neck muscles soon spasm and burn, so I draw up my knees and lean on them. A twirl of the focus ring on the lenses brings the creek's eddies, bubbles, and globs of spume into shattering clarity. In the middle of the creek, water sheets over a barely submerged stone. A soot-gray bird lands and does four or five knee bends before flying downstream. I recognize the American dipper, or ouzel, that spends its life on mountain streams like this, diving underwater for fish.

Time creeps by. Except for my peephole to the creek, I'm encased in a cocoon of willows. Before I'm aware of it, my mind starts to wander into a familiar chain of what-ifs. What if a grizzly bear decides to come down for a drink in the creek right here? What if, just beyond that bend in the creek, are a moose cow and calf? They could charge me where I am and trample me to a bloody pulp. What if I drop my pants to pee in the bushes and some animal creeps up behind me and nails me—and later on the guys find me, bottom up, again a bloody pulp?

I laugh at the fears tapping at my inner window. I've merely traded civilization fears for wilderness fears. I come from a place where my greatest daily threat was getting into a fender-bender on my way to work. In the background, of course, were those vague city fears: Some psychopath might sneak up from behind and nab you, an addict might break into your house and steal your stuff. Now, if someone were to enter my dilapidated, rodent-infested Park Service trailer, they would find nothing I couldn't live without. So as one set of fears is allayed, another is conjured up to take its place: bears in the woods, moose tramplings. I'm sure I'm the only S&RM employee who even thinks about such things. Some people have no imagination.

A doughy cloud rambles across the sun, graying my willow glade. I set down the binoculars to rub my neck, and then my breath catches. *Ho, what's this?* A brown motion, bobbing near the opposite shore, moving downstream with the creek flow. I slowly bring up the binocs. There's a duck, a mother, dun-colored with a white disk behind her eye, followed by six similarly patterned young. Seven harlies!

As soon as my hand aims for my radio holster, the mother spots me and turns, signaling for her brood to follow. I unsnap the holster and yank out the Motorola.

"*Tim!*" I rasp. "I see some! A mom and six kids." I'm so shaky I have to scramble-grab the radio to keep my sweaty hands from flinging it into the creek.

"Cool. I'm on my way."

"They're headed upstream," I say.

"I'll stay in the water and herd them back down." Then, a minute later, "I see 'em. They're just chillin' under a rock overhang."

Julian's barely audible squawk is next: "I'll string up an Avinet."

I stay hidden in the willows, my breath coming in shallow puffs. When I project ahead to what these ducks are about to endure, a grainy heat floods my ribcage. *No, no, no.* They're in their home, in this wild and far-flung place, doing what harlequins do, living life—and we're about to ambush them and shatter their world.

The ducks float downstream past me. Then Tim appears, a lumbering galoot, sloshing through the creek behind them. I slip into the creek to join him.

"Let's put up another net," he says, "in case they turn back."

He hands me a plastic bag, and I withdraw a bundle of soft, black netting. We tie off the top ends of the net to two sturdy willow trunks, one on each shore, and anchor the bottom edge underwater with stones. The ducks are now swimming between Julian's net and ours. The young can't fly yet, so they're trapped. We herd them downstream.

My heart wrenches when I round a bend and see all seven ducks flapping helplessly in Julian's net. *Poor babies.*

I watch how Tim clamps his hands around the mother's wings, disentangles her from the net, then slips her into a cloth bag that Julian holds open. Using the same technique, I cup one of the ducklings in my hands and wangle it free of the net. *"Forgive me,"* I whisper. Its tiny paddle-feet quake as I release it into the bag.

One by one, we fish the ducks from the bag to weigh, sex, and band them. Tim does the sexing, flipping them upside-down in his lap to poke around for the recessed sex organs. "I know, I know," he says as one youngster struggles, "I wouldn't want someone turning me upside down and sticking me in the butt either." He chuckles as he continues, "You'll be fine. All your siblings had to go through this, and now it's your turn. Didn't your mother warn you about us?"

While Julian takes down the nets, I hold a young harlequin duck in my hands for Tim to clip on a leg band. This baby is a bundle of squirmy brown down with a stubby bill. Straining warm against my palms, it plops a milky slurry of anxiety-induced poop in my lap. I resist the urge to cradle it against my heart and murmur, "There, there, baby. You'll be okay."

When we've finished recording the data, Tim cuddles the bag in his arms and crouches into the water with it. When he opens the end, the ducks tumble out, scatter, and regroup, then paddle downstream into the shadows.

What gives us the right? At what cost do we gain information?

Earlier this summer, Roy Jones, the biologist at the National Elk Refuge, down the road from Grand Teton, told me about his elk calf research. Puffing out his chest, he explained that he and his research team swoop down in a helicopter over a group of cows and calves. When they get close enough, the cows run away, while the calves cower down under the draft from the blades. Then it's easy for him to jump out of the chopper and snap radio collars on them.

"My *god*," I said, clutching my stomach in horror. "Talk about stress . . ."

Roy shrugged and stroked the crown of his head as if there were still hair there. "We're getting great information," he said.

It's so yang, I thought.

If we had more person-power, could we do this less intrusively and still glean all this gilded scientific data we crave? Native Americans learned about wildlife through patient tracking and diligent observation. True, they didn't know the exact weight of a harlequin duck. But does knowing the weight, in grams, of a harlequin duck justify the physiological damage caused by the explosion of stress hormones through its terrified body? Does human knowledge of a harlequin's weight help the species survive over time? Or does it merely enable researchers to gloat over their achievements at scientific conferences?

What if we adopted the Native American hands-off approach? What if we said no more gadgets, no more handling, no more radio collars, antennas, leg bands? Just sit. Watch. Take notes. Blend.

As wildlife biologists, we have a rare opportunity, but also a responsibility, to flow through the wild places with care and reverence. But it's not enough for us. We force too hard, disrupting the natural rhythms of the very wilderness we seek to protect. We are human after all, not wild animals, and controlling wildness is still a respected means of succeeding in the human world.

It's past sundown by the time we roll up the nets, with five and a half miles left to hike out. On the way, we get sidetracked in a huckleberry patch, dropping handfuls of berries into an empty Nalgene water bottle. Night comes, and we walk back in the tree-sifted light of an egg-shaped moon.

I'm especially uneasy hiking through prime grizzly habitat at night, reeking of huckleberry juice, but we stay together for the remainder of the hike back to the canoes. Through glass-smooth water, we paddle along a path of reflected silver moonlight, across the Moose Creek outlet.

Thwack! Water splashes over the gunwales. I hold my paddle in midair, whip my head side to side.

Thwack! Thwack!

All around us, beavers, annoyed at our presence, slap the water with their tails and dive under our canoes. I twist around, share a hushed laugh with Tim. His eyes beam through the moonlight.

We're stressing these beavers simply by passing through their habitat. Could we truly just sit, watch, and record without leaving some human mark in the wilderness?

Back at the cabin, Tim passes out bottles of home brew and fires up the stove. We cook up and toss down an indiscriminate hodgepodge of antelope sausage, rice, carrots, zucchini, potatoes, cranberry sauce, and oatmeal cookies.

At midnight in my sleeping bag, my limbs jerk as disjointed images tumble through my mind. Sapphire skies shot through with rockets of spruce and fir. A dipper squatting on a creek rock. The tiny moon behind a harlequin's eye.

Deep in sleep, my coworkers murmur baby-animal noises from nearby bunks. I hear an owl hoot through the night, wind whisper through aspen leaves, a tail smack on water. Then I swear I hear the pad of a bear's foot on the creek bed as the weight of a gargantuan harlequin duck bears down on my conscience.

Six

In February 2009, newspapers, magazines, websites, blogs, and at least one radio broadcast carried news of the demise of an atypical celebrity. He expired in a tiny corner of southwest Montana, but some of the reports concerning his death were in places as far away as Seattle. There was a spike in the viewing of his YouTube footage (and, yes, his Facebook page), and the event rated mention by the Associated Press.

This well-known local playboy died after apparently becoming entangled in a fence in the mountain-hemmed environs of Gardiner, Montana (population 900 people and 600 dogs). It might seem a little outrageous, even in the rural West, for a popular public figure to die in such a manner, but this was no ordinary star to begin with: The celebrity in question was none other than Elk Number Six, often called simply "Six" by fans and foes alike.

I was living in Missoula, Montana, when my phone rang. Then the texts started arriving, followed by e-mails. By that evening, people I hadn't spoken with in years were calling to tell me about Six's death.

One might rightly wonder why an unemployed biologist living in a graduate student's basement would receive such attention as the result of an elk expiring 300 miles away. I don't have many claims to fame, and those that I do have are sufficiently dubious that I don't care to recall them. I can, however, make this assertion with confidence: I spent more time, eyeball to eyeball, with Elk Number Six than did any other human being.

I don't make this declaration lightly; hundreds of tourists watched this elk's aggressive antics in the Mammoth Hot Springs area of Yellowstone National Park. Additionally, his tendency to utilize certain yards in nearby Gardiner, Montana, as winter daybeds—as well as the tacitly tolerated hand-feeding of elk and deer in town—ensure that a select number of locals have indeed been in very close proximity to this particular elk at times.

Having said that, I still make the claim that I spent more time with Six than anyone else. Because for most of the nine years I rangered at Yellowstone National Park, the arrival of crisp September nights and shortening days meant one thing: Elk would appear in Mammoth Hot Springs for the rut. And my life would not be the same until November.

Elk-rutting in the HQ area was nothing new when I arrived in Mammoth. As bulls came into rut, they would arrive in search of cows who had been attracted to the well-manicured lawns of Fort Yellowstone for years. The same Kentucky Bluegrass that allowed picnicking tourists to avoid the reality of the arid intermountain West became increasingly attractive to elk as the surrounding natural landscape dried and died. The additional fact that those same crowds of people also generally deterred visits from grizzlies and wolves made Mammoth just too good for the elk to pass up.

It is not a common scenario. In fact, there are few other places on the continent—Banff National Park being another—where people can step out of a minivan and into an elk rut. Indeed, as many hunters complained to me over the years, it's often difficult to get close to a rutting bull in the backcountry. The rut, then, was another example of the wild allure of Yellowstone.

There was the occasional warning to a tourist overly eager to pet an angry, urine-soaked bull, and every so often, an aggressive bull would arrive and stir up some chaos. Generally though, the Mammoth rut wasn't considered a major event.

That changed with the arrival of the bull who would become Six.

If you don't know who Six was, or why he was famous—infamous—then you're obviously not one of the thousands of tourists who witnessed his antics during the four years of his reign. Six was famous for chasing people and damaging cars. He was dehorned (an inaccurate term for sawing off an elk's antlers) twice—the only elk who has rated such treatment in the long history of Yellowstone National Park. The first time we darted him, it was the result of Six goring one man, narrowly missing another, and doling out thousands of dollars in property damage to visitor-, employee-, and government-owned vehicles.

It was on one fateful September morning in 2004 that Six received his numerical moniker. Still relatively anonymous, he was in the process of mounting a receptive cow when Kerry Gunther—the park's storied Bear Management Officer—fired a drug-filled dart into his hip. The drugs began to take effect, and within a few minutes, the massive bull lay down, passing into unconsciousness and history.

We monitored the breathing and pulse of this aromatic, 800-pound animal as the bone saw worked its way through each of his antlers. Because of certain legal requirements regarding wildlife drugs, the National Park Service was obligated to place an ear tag on any elk who had been darted. This informed hunters—who could legally take elk outside the park—that the meat of their trophy bull might just be full of powerful tranquilizers. Someone reached into the capture kit and took out the plastic bag full of cattle ear tags. From that bag came a red tag with a 6 on it, and the neighborhood was never the same.

A reversal agent was administered to counteract some of the immobilization drug mixture. Those who were assembled withdrew. The ungulate biologist, Dr. PJ White, and Kerry left technicians Travis Wyman, Lori Roberts, and myself to observe Six's recovery. On the lookout for physiological complications, we also scanned the area for the bigger risk: other bulls. As large and powerful as Six was, competing bulls would recognize this drug-induced period of weakness and would try to kill him.

I clearly remember the three of us sitting in the truck, chatting and watching Six slowly recover. We all knew him to be a big, tough customer, but there had been other such elk in the history of the park: Number Ten was at that time the largest and most well known of the Mammoth elk. As far as we were concerned, we had just tagged another bull elk. None of us had any inkling of what the future held.

Following our reluctant dehorning operation, Six's notoriety skyrocketed. That day marked the beginning of the Era of Six. The park received e-mails and calls from the public and from news outlets. PJ fielded calls from local newspapers and radio stations in California asking about The Elk That Hits Cars or The Elk Who Gored That Guy. Some people were outraged that we didn't kill him; the animal was a menace, they said. Other people were equally outraged by our cruelty: lacking the most basic understanding of cervid biology, they believed that we had permanently removed his antlers.

"Oh, no, ma'am, they grow back every year." I found myself explaining this several times a day.

"That can't be right," she objected. "Those antlers are too big. An animal couldn't possibly regrow them every single year. Besides, how will he defend himself against the wolves?"

Calculating the risks, I began the fascinating but often unwelcome evolutionary explanation that elk antlers are predominantly used for display—for showing off to females, intimidating other males. As weapons, they are most often wielded against other bulls.

"Certainly," I said, "they *can* be used in defense, but that's not really . . . "

"That can't be right," she repeated, interrupting. "Those antlers are *pointed*; anyone can see that they use them to stab things like wolves."

"How do cows defend themselves?" I asked gently. "They don't have antlers. What about bulls in velvet? The thin skin covering their antlers at that time is very sensitive."

She clearly cared for my explanations about as much as she cared for wolves, for in response she huffed and walked away.

The next fall, to the collective dismay of many administrators, Six returned to Mammoth. Suffice it to say that he immediately chose to reprise his bad-boy role: more chasing people, more dents, more broken car windows. I received the directive to dehorn him again. The drama took place over several days, but during that time, strangers began calling me by name, pleading "don't do it." Others, presumably with the opposite opinion, followed my daily movements with video cameras at the ready.

I darted Six for a second time on a cold September morning in 2005. Aware of the folks tailing me, I waited until he followed some cows behind a building and out of view. Pleased with my discreet plan, I watched as he began to feel the effects of the drugs, which must have been a familiar sensation by that time. True to his contrary nature, Six staggered around the building and into full view of the assembled video cameras before collapsing. Travis and I worked him up—relieving him of his antlers once more—and protected him as he recovered.

His second darting made Six even more popular. Although I've never seen any pictures or video footage of the event, that day somehow established, in the eyes of many, my personal association with him. From then on, some of Six's dedicated paparazzi and groupies would seek me out each season—sometimes knocking on my front door—to get the latest updates on their favorite elk.

He became as close to a rock star as any native ungulate has likely ever been. His name began to appear on websites, online message boards, and blogs. He got his own Facebook page. Visitors began to ask for him. Merchants in Gardiner were telling people to be sure to see Six when they went into the park. Inspired by Six, the BBC sent a photographer to get video of Mammoth elk chasing people. Postcards of him dehorned appeared, captioned ANGER MANAGEMENT, YELLOWSTONE STYLE. Dozens of people set up chairs in the beds of their pickup trucks, tailgating until long after sunset to watch him chase cows and battle bulls.

It was during one of those spectator events that I was standing near one of the various parking lots in which I spent the majority of my time during the rut. I noticed a young couple encouraging their little girl to walk over to me. After some effort on their part, she toddled over. Glancing back at her beaming parents, she looked up at me and asked, "Wheas numbah six?"

Well, I thought, *it's finally happened. He's not just any rock star, he's Elvis.* And for better or worse, I was his manager. Four years after he first rose to prominence, Six's fame had become multigenerational. His name was known far and wide. I should note that, officially, the park does not name animals. The administration is very clear that the National Park Service does not wish to anthropomorphize wildlife.

I, on the other hand, admit guilt in utilizing some highly descriptive—and unprintable—designations with regard to Six. That's because our association had reverberated into my life in ways I never expected. There were years when Six and I weren't more than a few blocks apart for months. I lost sleep when he circled my residence, bugling *all* night. My relationships with friends and one lover were temporarily damaged by Six. I lost weight. Sometimes I damn near lost all perspective.

I was the one who got the calls when he was standing in front of the Mammoth Hotel, irrationally slashing at anything and anyone that came close—people hated him.

I was the one who got the calls when he was limping around Mammoth, or when he was in Gardiner, in some alley or yard that was judged to be uncomfortably close to the hunt zone boundary—people worried about him.

Over the years, I was with Six when he was frenetic from hormonal rage, and when he was sedated. I was with him when he was healthy, and when he was injured. I was there when he was king of the proverbial Mammoth hill, and I was there when he was beaten. I saw him during the zenith of his aggressive behavior toward the throngs of unwary humans, and perhaps most importantly, I witnessed him display remarkable acts of regal indifference and tolerance toward those same crowds.

For all the Six stories people will tell—and people do love to spin yarns about him—few if any of those tales will be poetic reminiscences of the time he did *not* charge into a group of clueless elderly people who inexplicably found themselves standing next to him. Nor will they talk about the time he charged—but did *not* contact—a man talking on his cell phone who never even noticed the massive bull elk who could have easily driven an antler through man's body, had he so chosen.

No, Six is famous for his tendency to damage cars and chase people.

Six had passed from reality into the realm of folklore years before his death. As such, the myth of Elk Number Six grew all out of proportion to the animal. Every day during the rut, someone would come up to me and tell me something new about Six—he'd killed a man a few years ago, he'd been shipped off to Canada but made his way back.

Stories like this will endure, and Six will likely always be famous for his aggression. But the ironic truth is that his fame was a result of his tolerance. Six was figuratively born in the wildland-urban interface, of which Mammoth Hot Springs is a tenuous, but instructive, example. His notoriety wasn't solely due to his belligerence; any number of bulls are probably as willing and as capable of inflicting damage on people and property. Six's fame came from the stage where he played out that violence: He charged, punctured, dented, and threatened amid the paved streets and buildings of a pedestrian mall packed with loud, unpredictable, and often unwary crowds of humans.

If not exactly enamored of mankind, Six was undeniably comfortable around humanity. During the rut—the most difficult time of an adult elk's life—Six spent most of his time in the vicinity of a busy gift shop, a post office, and a fast-food restaurant. He stood in the road as cars and RVs rumbled by, less than an arm's length away. He drowsed next to sidewalks teeming with Boy Scouts and tour groups. How many other wild animals—much less hormonally enraged bull elk—would tolerate such close proximity to so much human activity for so long? As "wild" as people considered him, Six was, in the parlance of wildlife management, habituated.

In conclusion, my familiarity with Six and his history lead me to make one more audacious assertion: His death was not, as some observers called it, a freak accident. It was a predictable outcome of his close association with humanity and our constructed environment. Over the years, I have seen many cases of habituated wildlife, from sea turtles and dolphins to coyotes and bears. Almost always, the animal eventually meets a premature demise, be it from carelessness around armed humans, coronary heart disease from eating our food, or being hit by a car. Six should have died on a snowy ridgeline in the company of winter cold and a mountain lion, or simple infirmity, but he died tangled in a fence behind a motel, because that is representative of how he lived.

If I'm right, and I spent more time with Six than anyone else, then it stands to reason that I learned more from Six than anyone else. I suspect that all the experiences he bestowed on me in his distinctly inelegant way will take a lifetime to truly understand and appreciate. For that, I publicly thank the glorious, majestic, infuriating pain in the ass who was Elk Number Six.

Thinking Like Water

Matthew Bowser

Atop the world's largest supervolcano, I labored away the summer months of the past five years on a backcountry trail crew. The exterior of Yellowstone National Park bubbles with a subtle, weird beauty that reflects the forever-changing universe buried underground. Just beneath its mountainous crust, a colossal cauldron of magma boils in silence, waiting for its moment to breathe deeply again. The volcano's influence above ground is apparent in every hot spring, fumarole, mud pot, and geyser—constant, steaming reminders of the uncertain future that resides below.

In 1988, wildfires roared through the park, burning over a third of the landmass. The epic megafires left behind an apocalyptic landscape of dead-standing lodgepole pine forests that make visitors grimace and wonder why the Park Service doesn't cut them down. Often neglected from their field of vision, however, are the billions of small, new-generation trees that are compacted, competing, and climbing together in a race for the sky.

Amid this backdrop of regrowing panorama and percolating creation, I dug earth with pick and shovel as a member of the West District Trail Crew (WDTC). At the same time, I dug further into myself, attempting to break through darkened crust and discover the superheated core that lies beneath.

Before I came to Yellowstone, being a trail worker was already my default profession. I got to work in amazing, wild country from Vermont to Alaska and to be a part of crews that did meaningful work in the woods. The seasonal lifestyle became an addiction that took a strong hold of me. Summers were filled with long days and demanding work that left me completely exhausted. Come autumn, I was ready to be out of the woods. Winter was a time to immerse myself in creative expression and to feed the spirit through music, video production, and skiing. But every April, the spring winds would blow off the mountains, whispering, summoning me back into the hills toward a job again.

By the time I got to Yellowstone, I'd spent six years doing and enjoying trail work, and my plan at that point was to continue on with it until I figured out what I "really wanted to do." Ironically, when my yellow brick road led me to the backcountry trails of Yellowstone, I came to the realization that I was already doing what I wanted in life: saving trails.

To understand what I mean when I state, "saving trails," you must first understand trail work. The commonly held perception of a trail crew involves a group of twentysomethings who clear blown-down trees during the day and rage with handles of whisky at night. While this impression is not entirely false, the occupation is much more involved. It's a physically demanding job that taxes the limits of muscle exertion. For ten-hour days, in eight-day-straight stints, we hauled heavy building materials and crushed yards of rock with sledgehammers to construct paths that would endure several years of foot traffic and stock use. It's a sweat-logged labor of love that throws mud in your face and leaves you bruised and bloodied.

In a park as large and popular as Yellowstone, trails are

the best backcountry management tool available. By keeping the legions of hikers and stock animals that traverse through the park on a single route, the Park Service avoids a multitude of haphazard individual avenues that scar hillsides and trash watersheds. A trail builder's job is to establish a tread that is safe and up to standard, one that screams to forest visitors, "Hey! Go this way!" Trail crews accomplish this by providing a pathway that is hardened, sheds water, and keeps erosion in check.

More simply stated, we build trails so that people don't get their feet wet. Even in this day and age of triple Gore-Tex–lined underwear, hikers see a tiny mud puddle in the trail and walk around it. As more and more travelers follow along and take that bypass, the puddle morphs into an abysmal quagmire that *is* fitting for fancy underwear. Our aim on the trail crew is to restore these muck holes—and to do our best to prevent them from occurring in the first place.

The job, at its most basic level, consists of being able to read the land. The eyes of a trail worker evaluate the existing tread and the adjacent surroundings that are susceptible to erosion. Water flows by taking the path of least resistance, so we begin to think like water in all its forms: rain, snowmelt, seeps, streams, and rivers. We calculate the grade of the trail and assess the slope of the hillside to estimate the potential water damage.

The simple exercise of thinking like water puts you in a deep relationship with the immediate environment. While standing still, hugging the land with your eyes and envisioning a year's worth of precipitation, you are remarkably grounded to a patch of earth.

Upon recognition of the land-water correlation, the trail crew sets out to shape the soil and construct devices that divert water and retain existing tread. On a designated trail, the average hiker walks over countless such contraptions without giving much thought to their intended purpose. The thingamabobs they see during their hikes have names: water-bars, check-dams, retainers, turnpikes, and, in more obvious situations, bridges. They are made of native rock or wood, and without them, a trail turns into a trench, mountains dissolve into streams, and habitat vanishes.

Few jobs remain in modern-day American society that take place in the woods. There are even fewer still where work is actually accomplished on a forest and the results are so readily measurable. The reward for performing these meaningful measures doesn't come with a dollar sign attached. The reward is not a paycheck but a title: "trail dog." It's a term of endearment and respect in our profession, given to someone who has spent at least seven seasons living and working on trails. A trail dog might have yet to encounter all of the possible muddied situations a trail has to offer, but he or she has been around long enough to formulate a knowledgeable response. It is not a label that is thrown around aimlessly amongst the crew. One must earn the title much like a gangster in a Mafia film is "made." The term has been handed down through generations of trailblazers. "Trail dog" denotes a benchmark that, once achieved, is more satisfying than a paycheck.

My first season on the WDTC in Yellowstone was the year I became a trail dog. By that time, I had acquired seven years' worth of skills and was kicking down the knowledge by leading volunteer groups. However, both the job and I were falling into a mundane, daily routine. The sun shone every morning along with the complacency in my smile. How exactly was I contributing toward the good in the world? If I was going to continue saving trail in the future, I had to unearth a deeper meaning to the vocation—one that would enable me to reinvent myself and to redefine trail work.

After the '88 fires, Yellowstone trail crews began constructing bridges to address any mud puddle and every miniscule stream-crossing they found. As a result of the fires, an endless supply of "kiln-dried" wood surrounded their work sites, and they used it exclusively in their construction. Twenty years later, nearly every one of those bridges was rotten, falling apart, and in need of replacement. There was now an epidemic of bridge disintegration on the west side of the park, and the leader and heart of the WDTC—Captain Hook—faced an enormous challenge.

Captain Hook did not get his nickname as a result of an arm amputation. (Although this past year, while at a local bar, playing a video-poker machine, a ram head fell off its wall mount and crushed his hand. But that's a different story altogether.) Hook is a rare, caring, enduring leader who radiates from his unselfish core all attention and all positive energy toward the crew. His judgments as a trail boss are carefully thought out and democratically discussed among the crew. His methods mandate that trail issues be resolved through permanent solutions and not mere Band-Aids. And the concerns he faced with the rotten-bridge dilemma weighed heavy; after all, his decisions would have long-lasting implications.

To rebuild, bridge for bridge, was the old way of doing business. It was the preferred solution back in the day when trail workers had more time and Yellowstone had fewer hikers. But these days, the park is a premier backcountry destination: Every other issue of *Backpacker* magazine illustrates the wonders of "secret Yellowstone hikes," and the masses follow. With this dramatic rise in visitation came an increased need for maintenance on those trails that are no longer a secret. By spending an abundance of time building a bridge on one problem spot, we'd be allowing far more destruction to occur elsewhere due to a simple lack of maintenance. Bridge construction is time-consuming, expensive, and nearly impossible these days due to a new ordinance that forbids the cutting of green trees in Yellowstone. More importantly, no matter how well conceived and well constructed, all bridges made of wood will one day fall victim to rot and will eventually fail.

The design of trail structures has changed little since the time when footpaths for travel transformed into micro-highways for recreation. Yet the WDTC began experimenting on a small scale with a Hook-inspired device called the "crushed-dip-drain." It was first used in places where narrow streams crossed a trail. It consists of two retainers on either side of the stream as well as one on the downstream portion, where water exits the trail. The retainers are composed of either rock or wood. (Yes, wood. When wood is completely submerged in water or buried underground, the rate at which it rots slows dramatically. It is only when wood is exposed to the elements—cycling through periods of wet and dry—that it decomposes rapidly. In fact, an entire sector of the Pacific Northwest timber industry is dedicated to dredging lakes and rivers to harvest old-growth wood that has been hibernating under water for decades.) Between the retainers, large amounts of rock are crushed to form a hardened surface. This permits the water to flow freely over the golf ball–sized rocks while allowing stock animals to cross without getting bogged down in the stream or destroying the native vegetation along its banks.

The walkover device has structural integrity and lasting functionality. And it is attractive from an economic standpoint since it takes one-fifth of the time as constructing a bridge. More importantly, the simple design produces the unintentional benefit of concealing the apparatus within the trail, as opposed to the obtrusive aesthetic of bridges in a wilderness setting.

No two crushed-dip-drains look alike. Originality is inherent, because the design is tweaked and adapted to individual sites.

Each one attains a dimension of its own, determined by its purpose and setting.

The crushed-dip-drain was so effective that it eventually became the exclusive replacement structure for bridges in Yellowstone. To date, over forty bridges have been removed and supplanted with the innovation. The WDTC revisited the original prototypes that were implemented, and discovered that they were still functioning flawlessly.

Hook's creation not only delivered a practical method for bridge substitution, but also reinvigorated my passion for saving trails. My job as a trailblazer was no longer a fight to build above and around water but to flow with it. I seized upon the subtle aspect that the crushed-dip-drain embodied and began applying it to everything I constructed in the woods. I wanted to make *all* obvious structures disappear completely—to build trails that performed for decades without erosion, and in which all traces of work were buried, hidden from sight. The end result of my inspired tactics would appear as though no work had been done at all.

The newfound intention of my work became an endeavor to empower people. Hikers with thoughts free from distractions (bridges) on the trail could wander any way they chose in their minds, while their feet followed unaware in strict accordance to my direction. The symbolic implications of this were mind-blowing to my soul-searching spirit. I believed I had established a new breed of trail dog: one that attempted to provide an unnoticed platform to bridge the gap between wilderness and humans—without a bridge. I called this distinct pedigree of trail worker a "guide dog." Trail work had entered a contemporary and delicate realm of expression. It was a sophisticated art form of gift giving, providing the paths on which others might uncover a genuine perception of themselves and the place on the world in which they walk.

With a clear mind, pure intent, and time, I was once again absorbed by Yellowstone. The longer I stayed in the woods, the deeper my connection rooted into the unraveling network of forest life. Hidden rhythms and unnoticed sounds now announced themselves daily and became as commonplace as the clock on an office wall. It was not like some kind of hippie bumper sticker with musical notes that read, "BE IN TUNE WITH NATURE." It was being with Earth. I felt a direct link between the volcano that churned beneath my feet and the wish-fueled fire that burned in my heart. Every night, my bedroom ceiling was an endless spray of glowing sky that seemed to suggest just how fortunate I was. I understood that I was participating in the same time and space as the park. Everything had been elevated to an almost holy level.

Not everyone on the WDTC shared my vision of a seamless union between work and land, but we were all united in our admiration of the park, and we all wanted what was best for Yellowstone: sustainable protection. Our setting brought us together and shaped the community that we formed. We were dependent upon each other for both survival and happiness in the wilderness. Spending extended periods of time living and working in the woods together, we forged enduring personal relationships. I may have been the only "guide dog" on crew who envisioned Hook's crushed-dip-drain as the gateway to higher consciousness, but collectively, we built them.

Year after year, more knowledge was shared between the yellow rock and I as friendship turned into commitment. I discovered more efficient ways of building invisible trails, and in return, I was paid in prism-inspired sunsets. The reconstructive work I performed on the park's trails led to the cosmic therapy of my spirit. I got to live and work immersed in a breathing magic that consistently reminded me how wealthy I was. I learned to let my thoughts gravitate into my core, like the waters flowing down their paths of least resistance. When I was in Yellowstone, I became Earth, and I did not exist without digging into it. The more I gave of myself, the more of myself the park gave to me.

An Admirable Hard Start

Seth Slater

It was the last summer he would have use of his legs, and he used them that season to habitually launch himself into the saddle. It was a jaunty movement, that casual boot-leather step from ground to stirrup, followed by a gracefully expansive upward arc and a firm seating, which, when done properly, produced a weary creak of protestation from beneath the buttocks.

Watching Pat was like falling in love with an idea not yet fully formed. At the time, we only knew that we were drawn to the sound of creaking saddle leather. That we wanted to live lives of casual, jaunty grace. That we wanted to play cowboy.

That's why we were there. City kids barely into our twenties mostly, wanting for several months to be transformed into wranglers and trail guides—hired hands for a mule-packing outfit at the base of a 9,000-foot summit, halfway between the towns of Lee Vining and Bridgeport, along California's Highway 395. Before the season was out, we would cumulatively cover more than 800 miles on horseback—with teams of pack mules trailing behind us in long strings—through Yosemite National Park's beautifully rugged southeast corner and the expansive Hoover Wilderness, which lay to its east.

In retrospect, Pat's swing into the saddle may have been too theatrically calculated to properly qualify as one demonstrating genuine ease. The truth that summer was that, collectively, we cultivated and drew from a whole repertoire of gestures characterized by an air of exaggerated restraint that were used to impress ourselves and each other. Among us that summer was Pete, the dye-headed surfer and part-time band member who arrived rail-thin and incapable of lifting much more than the weight of his electric guitar, let alone a bale of hay one third his size. Scott from Tennessee was accustomed to rolling hills and wide-open spaces, and he felt claustrophobic in the woods, surrounded by trees—a difficult situation to avoid when living and working in one of the most extensive conifer stands on the continent. Little Lauren's worldly knowledge had been shaped almost exclusively by church sermons, political-science lectures, and sorority songs. I, on the other hand, had arrived ready for high adventure with the best traits of my fellows already well at hand: I possessed Pete's strength, Scott's knowledge of woodsmanship, and Little Lauren's wealth of experience beyond suburbia, having recently graduated from a respectable school that taught me how to expertly edit articles for the school newspaper by rearranging dangling modifiers into more grammatically acceptable alternatives. I wasn't even sure what the differences were between a horse and a mule. There were others among us, but for the most part, we all had similar qualifications.

We walked with a slight hint of bowlegged swagger, just enough to convince that any other form of locomotion was a practical impossibility. To fill a gap in conversation, we spat lazily and never into the breeze. In closing a distance, we'd pass one another with a curt nod—a small downward movement, like a cowboy burdened with chores—never with chin tilted upward, like a carefree college kid from the city might. We'd touch a finger or two to the brim of our hats, ever mindful not to speak unnecessarily, lest a "Hey, dude" or "How's it goin'" escape out of campus habit.

In deference to our notions of the Western work ethic, unless it was on horseback, we tended to avoid sitting. A weary lean against fence rails or a hunkering, loose-kneed squat was preferred. Only when circumstances clearly indicated its necessity was sitting even considered. And then, it was believed permissible only after giving a brief but deliberately noticeable look around to satisfy that all was in order, that nothing a seasoned wrangler would leave undone remained. The sitting itself was most effective when accompanied by a beleaguered look plainly suggestive of patient resignation. Whenever compelled to acquiesce to the sitting idea, the resulting pose was one in which all limbs were arranged at square, solid angles.

Strangely, all of this posturing took place as a natural and unconscious manifestation of a longing we each felt. We were impatient for a competence we hadn't yet genuinely cultivated— not by a long shot. As a shortcut, we did things the way Pat did them. We carried ourselves the way he did, because if any of us had ever stopped to think about it, Pat was who we wanted to be. And so we studiously watched him on those upward arcs into the saddle. Seeing his ever-present, enviable aura of ease, we thought we were watching John Wayne or Clint Eastwood heading off to roam the range.

Pat was from New Jersey, and he spoke with good humor and a quick smile in an unrefined twang that betrayed his origins in a working-class neighborhood far to the east. But in his well-worn black cowboy hat and with his lean, muscular physique, he looked every bit the part he had come here to play. It was his second season as a packer, so we all looked up to him. We needed to. There were more experienced hands to learn from, to be sure, among the handful of seasoned pack-outfit veterans, trail bosses, or even the outfit owners themselves. But theirs was an experience born of many years' dedication to (and often an upbringing in) the wrangler life. Pat, on the other hand, was still one of us. The things he knew he'd learned in a single season, and if he could do it, so could we.

Livestock and paying customers were vital to the success of the outfit, and we novice packers were to become responsible for the safety and comfort of both. Unlike backpackers, who had to content themselves with lightweight, dehydrated meals, the comfort of our customers was largely seen to by the mules themselves. With their individual loads of up to 150 pounds apiece, they were able to furnish—in addition to cooking stoves, tents, and bedrolls—fine backwoods luxuries like T-bone steaks and raw vegetables kept fresh in coolers. On occasion, we even managed to dazzle customers with cartons of ice cream for a decadent backcountry dessert.

Our pack trips were, in fact, billed as gourmet camping excursions into some of the remotest regions of the Yosemite wilderness. Each year, Yosemite National Park plays host to some 3.5 million tourists, most of whom never venture beyond the seven square miles of Yosemite Valley that constitute only one percent of the park's total area. Mules and horses, as they always have in the West, dramatically alter conceptions of what is possible, and effectively open vast tracts of territory and entire vistas for exploration. Which meant, naturally, that we greenhorns had to learn—and quickly—to shed convincing pretense for actual competence if we were to be turned loose to ramble around in the woods with customers and livestock in tow.

The outfit owners and trail bosses had their work cut out for them early in the season. So did Pat. Techniques for catching horses and bailing hay had to be taught and learned. The fine art of balancing pack loads and tying knots—including the sinuous, load-securing diamond hitch—had to become second nature. Even learning to pick out individual mules from a herd of homogenous red- and brown-hued coats took some doing for most of us. At first, there were day rides and saddle sores. The bowlegged gaits we had assumed from the first became exaggerated and then, gradually, receded into something more tastefully subtle and real. Our forearms bronzed. Our hands, in spite of leather gloves, callused and cracked, became permanent repositories for dirt and grime. From time to time, over our shoulders, Pat would appear. He'd watch us struggle, working at some new task for a time, saying nothing. Then the corners of his mouth would draw downward for an instant, and his head would nod slowly, as if in appreciation of something newly discovered.

"That's one way to do it," he would venture in even tones. "Or . . . " he'd nudge us gently aside and demonstrate his method for a moment or two, always careful not to rob us of the task's completion, ". . . you could try something like that." Then he'd return the task to our hands and leave us, with a wink and the most encouraging of smiles, to our own good judgment. By the time the season's pack trips began, we had acquired something roughly resembling a working set of skills. Our abilities and our confidence grew as we left the sheltering confines of the pack station with increasing frequency, and pushed farther and farther into the surrounding wilderness.

Gentle slopes of shaded, brown woodland gave way to gray-green open spaces of subalpine forest whenever our pack trains climbed toward the rocky summit whose pass led down into the rich timberland of the Yosemite. In contrast to the parkland itself, the subalpine zone is a region of stunted beauty where stands of pines are dwarfed and exquisitely twisted by the wind. Islands of granite rock push through the topsoil and speak to the nature of the region's ancient origins. The granite of the Sierra Nevada Batholith is igneous—of the nature of fire, forged by intense heat. It is rock that has been violently belched from the depths. It comes from hidden places. All of us that season, in order to become packers, drew from inner reserves we had never consciously thought about. But before the summer was out, it was Pat, alone among us, who would be plucked from ordinary life and placed on the hammering forge of change.

For the rest of us, as the season progressed, rearrangements of a subtler sort made themselves manifest. Pete, the scrawny surfer, had grown bulging biceps, thanks in part to emulating Pat's backcountry predilection for push-up contests on the rocky outcrops overlooking our various campsites. Scott, the claustrophobic woodsman, had taken to long walks by himself beneath the pine canopy and would amble back to camp waxing poetic about the scent of trees and earth, or about the sensations of warm granite and wet grass. Little Lauren had developed a wrangler's eye for subtle changes in the behavior of the livestock under her care. And I, who had always prized the value of words above deeds, had come to understand the importance of actions in a world where things left undone meant that someone— horse, mule, or human—went hungry or cold at the end of a day.

Day after day, we traveled through a wilderness in which the land itself was literally out of place, formed by massive upheavals and dislocations. We entered Yosemite from the east and, over the course of ten days, made a wide horseshoe loop toward the park's southern border. Famed naturalist John Muir first remarked on the Yosemite's beautifully rugged "polished glacier pavements" in a series of articles penned in 1874 and 1875 for the *Overland Monthly*:

> "In the production of this admirable hard finish, the glaciers in many places flowed with a pressure of more than a thousand tons to the square yard, planing down granite, slate, and quartz alike, and bringing out the veins and crystals of the rocks with beautiful distinctness."

At one time, only Yosemite's highest peaks went unadorned by glacial ice. By their force, rock was bulldozed and mountains cloven. Then, as soaring temperatures freed them of interring ice, house- and car-sized boulders dropped out of the bottoms of melting glaciers onto massive slabs of pressure-burnished granite, resulting in surreal, backwoods, Stonehenge-like structures. Also in their retreating wake, glaciers left ponds and lakes, together with the high-alpine meadows through which we rode and camped.

All that summer, from our respective places in the long, winding line of horses and mules, we watched and learned from Pat. Our progress over the landscape could be observed in glimpses by lone backcountry hikers who, even from great distances, could see the train of pack animals, with their blue-tarpaulined loads, kicking up dust on the switchbacks of the trail. Sometimes they would pause long enough for us to catch up and chat with them, the backcountry version of dropping in on a neighbor in a wilderness where a person could hike or ride for days without encountering another human being. We picked our way around mountain ponds ringed even in July by remnants of winter snow, and we climbed up over rocky passes where the only sounds were of wind and shifting shale beneath animal hooves. We spent entire days traveling in uninterrupted stretches under shady boughs on mountain backs carpeted in pine, and in the evenings we camped by lakes or streams running though flower-dappled meadows, where the animals could be turned loose to graze and doze and graze again throughout the night.

We always made camp with several hours of light left to the day, so customers could hike or fish while we packers set up camp. Loads had to be unpacked, and animals tended to and turned out to pasture. Deadwood had to be gathered and cut for the evening's fire. Dinner would be prepared and coffee, in a tin pot placed directly on hot coals, would be set to roiling. And finally, tents had to be pitched. This last task was performed for the customers only. We packers preferred to toss a bedroll directly on the ground, since it both saved us work and gave us an unencumbered view of the spectacular night sky. It had the added advantage of making middle-of-the-night calls of nature a simple matter of padding barefooted down the length of the bedroll, unzipping, and issuing forth—so long as one had remembered to place that end of the bedroll in the downstream direction.

One morning, over a backcountry breakfast, a customer nodded toward Pat's empty bedroll and asked him why there was always a little pile of fist-sized rocks where he slept.

"Bears," he said simply.

"You're kidding. Are there really bears?"

"Sure, black bears. Didn't you notice the signs when we were riding in yesterday?"

"Signs?"

"Yeah, claw marks on the trees."

"Those were claw marks? I was wondering what those were. But those were as high as my shoulder—and I was sitting on a horse."

"They like to stretch."

"Oh." There was a contemplative pause. "So there are really bears here?"

"You bet."

Another pause. "Well, what do you do about 'em?"

"Throw rocks."

"Throw . . . but what if that doesn't work? What do you do then?"

There was a playful glint in Pat's eyes, and just the barest hint of a smile. "What do *I* do?"

"Yeah. I mean, I don't know anything about bears, so I'm asking—what do *you* do?"

Pat glanced around the breakfast fire at the customers' faces. The attention was undivided. "Well," he said with a grin, "I figure all I gotta do is outrun one of *you*."

Everyone laughed, and no one said another word about bears. But that night there was a pile of rocks by the entry flap of every tent—and also by every packer's bedroll. And so our learning went, all that summer.

Pat wasn't book smart, or cultured, or even particularly interested in anything that didn't involve horses or fast cars or some facet of athleticism or physical challenge. But he was a gifted and generous teacher nevertheless, and he played no small role that season in helping the rest of us come to feel at home in the woods.

But something was missing. He was a few years older than most of us, perhaps in his mid-twenties, and yet we each had something he lacked. Each of us wanted something out of life. Pete wanted to "make it" in a band. Little Lauren wanted to teach; I wanted to write. Pat, it seemed, had no sense of purpose. He spoke of no great dreams, no driving aspirations. And although it is certainly not uncommon in youth for many to find themselves without clear direction, there was something even more essential left wanting in Pat. He invited the unsettling impression that his sense of awe was somehow impaired. He possessed no bedrock of deep-held beliefs, no core of ideals. Nothing fascinated or perturbed him. Nothing impelled him toward contemplation or reflection. Grand backcountry vistas gratified but never beguiled him. It was as if all pursuits were mere diversion, as if—in spite of his presence in the wilderness— he was bereft of any true spirit of adventure. Perhaps things were simply too easy for Pat. Where, after all, was meaning to be found when all ventures were greeted with equal favor?

Until his accident, it never occurred to me that out of the lot of us, it was Pat alone who had reached a plateau, those long, flat stretches where the land remains horizontal and refuses to climb, however elevated it might be. Movie westerns are full of tablelands and plateaus—*mesas,* if you head far enough south. But such stagnant formations are the stuff of deserts and, as such, are relegated to barren locales. They call to mind the vast, arid tracts of places like New Mexico or Arizona. The Yosemite wilderness, on the other hand, is a place of cascading rock and soaring peaks, of glacial moraines and river-cut ravines. The Yosemite is no place for a plateau, and the land, containing none, perhaps discourages them in others.

Before white settlement in the 1800s, the Yosemite region was home to the Paiute, the Sierra Miwok, and the Ahwahneechee— peoples whose cosmologies told them that their lives were intimately tied to the spirits of the land. Over the years since his injury, I have wondered: Did the land itself sense something in Pat and come to a decision? Was he deliberately nudged, in some harsh gesture of grand irony, from his comfortable plateau of physical accomplishment, so that he might cultivate whatever lay beneath? Or was it merely a moment of youthful exuberance gone wrong that resulted in the permanent loss of the use of his legs? Pat's future, whatever it was to become after that summer, would call on him to draw from the hidden places, would demand reliance upon whatever inner strengths were to be found within his own cavernous, unexplored depths.

By season's end, a handful of us had been picked by the pack-outfit owners to lead a somewhat notorious bunch on a ten-day trip into the backcountry. The group was comprised entirely of men: several cops, a lawyer or two, and a respiratory therapist. They had been booking trips through the pack outfit every season for years. They weren't a bad bunch, the owners told us one evening, while we were all assembled around the pack station's dinner table between trips. It was just that, for this particular group, their annual outing represented an extended boys-night-out of sorts, and they tended to get a little rambunctious. An extra mule would be required just to haul the booze. And although the customers themselves wouldn't have objected to their company on the trail, the pack-outfit owners declared by executive order that female packers were strictly forbidden from taking part.

By the time we reached Smedberg Lake, at the southern tip of the park, we had only one day's ride ahead of us. The campsite was breathtaking, the pack season was winding down, and in the absence of women, a week of rough backwoods humor and running jokes had fostered a strong feeling of camaraderie among us. Perhaps it was the carefree atmosphere of cheery buoyancy that inspired Pat to ride an unbridled horse bareback through a meadow that evening. Perhaps he was the victim of overconfidence, or of a distracted horse. Perhaps if the sun hadn't been going down, he would have seen the dipping hollow of ground, and with a thigh nudged the horse out of its path. Perhaps if the horse hadn't been galloping. Perhaps.

Pat landed on his back on a hard knot of tree root. The wind was knocked from his chest in an audible, grunting sigh. We rushed toward him. He looked at us but couldn't speak. His arms scrabbled and clawed at the dirt. He managed to raise his shoulders, then his chest, from the ground. His eyes were wide and disbelieving as he gasped for air. His voice, when it came, was ragged and urgent. "I can't . . ." he began, but then he swallowed a rapid, shallow breath. First one, then another, and finally a third. "I can't . . . " he tried again. Each pull from his diaphragm produced a rasping wheeze. "Can't . . . feel my legs."

The meadow where Pat lay, although there were no remaining traces of it, had once been scorched by fire. So had every other patch of ground we'd traveled that trip and that season. After the granite-cleaving glaciers, and long, long after the sudden upheaval of bedrock from deep beneath the Yosemite, there was fire—and there still is. Everything that lives requires it. In the West—where conifer stands dominate but pine needles are slow to decompose—it is through fire that pines return their fertility to the soil and make way for the succession of plant species that follow. Rich, loamy substrates become home first to flowers, which yield to shrubs, which are overshadowed by leafy, rapidly growing deciduous trees, which ultimately are joined by pine-bearing conifers. When the ancient forests become brittle and dry, whenever they reach a natural climax of growth, fire transforms the land, insisting on an ever-upward climb of orderly succession.

And so, on his back in the wilderness, staring helplessly up at his companions, Pat lay on the fiery forge of change. The sun was going down, and we were a full day's ride from the pack station. Our position rendered cell phones useless. We made Pat as comfortable as we could. We urged him not to move, and we covered him in blankets in preparation for the oncoming cold of night. Then, stepping out of earshot, we held a backwoods council. There were several police officers and a respiratory therapist among us, but no one spoke of what rescuers so often refer to as the "golden hour"—that sheltering gossamer of time within which, if a hospital could be reached, a trauma victim might reasonably hope for a favorable outcome, and beyond which chances for recovery steadily declined. We decided to send Pete and another of our party out on horseback to ride through the night to the pack station, while the rest of us settled in for what turned out to be a nearly 15-hour stint of sleepless watchfulness, endless worry, and our collective best efforts to comfort and reassure Pat and each other.

We found an area we thought might make a suitable helicopter landing site and set up a triangular perimeter of signal fires, even though we wondered whether high elevation and nighttime winds might forestall a landing until daylight. A tent was pitched and its base cut out, so that the structure might be placed over Pat's prone body, should the menacing gray clouds overhead give way to rain. One of the police officers made his way as subtly as he could to a saddlebag, discreetly removed a gun, tucked it into his waistband, and covered it with his jacket. When one of the packers asked in a whisper what he was up to, he replied, "No bear's gonna get him on my watch." Finally, we brewed coffee and spoke in low tones and filled the silences with private thoughts and, undoubtedly in the case of some, prayers. Pat, for his part, bore up as one might expect he would. Although obviously at times frightened, he maintained his composure, complained little, and even managed a good-natured quip or two at his own expense.

No helicopter came during the night. When dawn arrived, we were straining to hear the distant sound of chopping rotor blades. The night wind was gone and the sky was clear, but we heard nothing. An hour later, fearing that something may have gone wrong with the night riders, we decided to send out two more on horseback. I was glad to be one of them, for it gave me something to do besides worry. The circuitous venture over winding trails only lasted for a round-trip total of several semi-hallucinatory hours.

Eventually, my riding companion and I encountered the two original night riders. They had been to the pack station, called for help, and were on their way back, together with several other members of the pack outfit. When we arrived back at the scene of the accident, a rescue helicopter had just landed—but not in the clearing adjacent to Pat. Unexpected weather at the lower altitudes had delayed takeoff, and by the time the helicopter had reached us, wind shear had become a factor in landing. The pilot couldn't make it to the clearing but had found another, in a more sheltered area, just a short stretch down the mountain.

That meant moving Pat on a litter down a winding trail made more narrow by the surrounding trees, as well as by our own swelling numbers. We must have made a clumsy gaggle that morning. I'm certain we had more hands on Pat's litter than it could reasonably accommodate. Some of us were forced into sideways crabwalks while others, eager for even an ineffectual single-handed hold, jockeyed for position from the outskirts. Precisely how we managed to maneuver without delivering any unpleasant jolts that might have aggravated Pat's injuries is beyond me. What was clear to me was that everyone there that day wanted to help carry Pat to safety, and did.

Looking up as the helicopter vaulted skyward, I recalled a tiny pine sapling I had seen on an afternoon ride through the backcountry. It had been tenaciously pushing its way up through a narrow crevice in a red-tinted terrace of burnished rock. I thought about the place in which we had come to find ourselves, of the sculpted rock of the Yosemite, of the cleaving pressures of glaciers and their painfully slow advance through time, of the scorching power of fire and the marching succession of plant life it left behind—from wispy flower to scruffy shrub to sturdy pine.

I looked about at my companions, at the tough young packers who just months before had constituted a fellowship of an entirely different sort. Outwardly recognizable, if a bit ragged and disheveled by our ordeal, we had been reorganized and transformed in our innermost parts. As the helicopter banked and receded, I wondered about what lay ahead for Pat and for us, and I thought that perhaps each of us had made not a finish, but an admirable hard start toward a life beyond the ancient valleys of granite uplifted.

The Traces You Leave

Nicole Sheets

On the road to Gardiner, Montana, I pass signs marking the Continental Divide. Waters from Canada to the Andes Mountains obey this line and empty east or west accordingly. I have never traveled farther west than the panhandle of Florida; I've emptied east all my life. A road sign marks the 45th parallel, exactly halfway between the equator and the North Pole. I imagine a globe and place myself, as a red dot, right on this latitude line. Hundreds of miles from my home, I find comfort in such precision.

This poorly paved road to Gardiner cuts through Yellowstone National Park. Any ranger will remind you that this park is no zoo. I gawk at elk loitering in the parking lot. Two bison mosey by a hotel. The animals were here first, rangers warn. I watch my step. I'm not entirely comfortable with the idea of invading someone else's home.

In Gardiner's uniform-fitting room, I contort my body to clean imaginary bathtubs. Room attendants receive two maroon shirts with the Yellowstone logo and two pairs of charcoal polyester pants. I try on two or three different sizes to make sure I don't get stuck with pants that ride up midscrub.

At the mandatory orientation program, a company representative tells me he is happy to have me on his team; I can experience the park like no tourist ever could; I'll learn a lot about myself and have fun. A slide presentation with peppy music shows smiling employees scooping ice cream and counting change at cash registers. I'm with a crowd of employees destined for housekeeping, and we cheer for each scene of bed-making or bathroom-cleaning. The surprised orientation man says the show rarely evokes much reaction, save for the occasional booing at the company's drug policy. I get a free pen, some hiking info, a pamphlet about the reintroduction of wolves, and the first stamp on my time card.

At the Old Faithful Snow Lodge, I spend most work days cleaning the outside cabins instead of the hotel. Rather than the wobbly upright carts that navigate a hotel's hallways, this work requires a wheelbarrow-sized molly. The training packet includes a diagram of an efficiently stocked molly; its tidy geometric blocks of bed linen and towels look like a city map. In the mornings at the linen shed, I arrange folded towels and sheets into neat stacks. In my first room or two, the sheets are still warm from the laundry in Gardiner, three hours away, and for a moment, I yearn to crawl back into my own bed.

At night, as I fall asleep, I make beds in my mind, unfurling full sheets and aligning their edges with the ends of mattresses. The process has a kind of origami flair: tucking the extra length of sheet beneath the head of the mattress, folding the wing-looking sides into tight miters like the crisp pocket hankies of dapper men. The second sheet I pleat, along with a coarse blanket, at the foot of the bed before I tug the bedspread to the standard one inch off the floor and tuck pillows into their cases like old-fashioned sandwich bags. Maybe it's a sign of my immersion in the work, this playback of the motions of the day. I also think of it as therapy.

Yellowstone rangers issue backcountry passes to the park's

summer workers. We watch a video about the dangers of camping in the park, including *Giardia lamblia* in the water and the year-round threat of snow. Even for day hikes, the rangers encourage us to travel in noisy groups to avoid catching bears and other wildlife by surprise.

I borrow all of my camping gear. I've never set up a tent, save for bed sheets strewn across the living room couches of my childhood. I have no plans to brave the wilderness solo.

Yellowstone isn't the place to push your limits, rangers say. Being alone isn't always a sign of strength.

My own mother is two time zones away, so Colleen makes a handy substitute. She has three children about my age, and she often asks about my well-being while inspecting my rooms. I struggle with fatigue, blaming it only half-seriously on Wyoming's altitude, figuring my body just isn't used to prolonged manual labor. Colleen consoles me that she too had trouble adjusting to the work, and that last summer she suffered a brief emotional breakdown outside a vacant cabin.

Colleen is radiant and sophisticated. It makes no sense for her to be relegated to a hotel housekeeping department, especially two summers in a row. She eats hummus in the employee dining room, but I picture her lounging on a veranda by the Mediterranean, fanning herself and eating olives. Drink a cup of water per room, she advises me on scorching days, but I know if I listen to her, I'd have to pee every twenty minutes, further slowing me down. I wait until the thirst gets painful or the room goes fuzzy blue before I bother unwrapping a plastic cup.

Often, while I'm cleaning, Colleen will breeze by to check my work. She sings about her Portuguese ancestors, or waves to me with a pillow shaped like a giant pink foot that she finds in a room, or fires a phrase *en español* for me to translate, or asks questions about my family. "What's your motivation?" she wants to know.

I ask whether she's referring to the sink I'm scrubbing or to life in general. That sink takes fifteen minutes as I stammer on about my spiritual goals, my type A personality, my rule-following childhood.

Colleen did not go to college, and I find this hard to believe too. Her glasses dangle from a chain around her neck, although one of the ear pieces has broken off, leaving a jagged stump by the right lens. As she peers over a list of vacant rooms or the minutes of a safety meeting, I picture her at a ritzy masquerade, holding up a Zorro-style mask by its one long stem, sequins and feathers laced around the eyeholes. Most mornings, Scott, her Yellowstone boyfriend, brings her yogurt and fruit on a large white plate from the Snow Lodge Restaurant. Scott is surly and I wonder what—apart from access to fruit plates and the ornate iguana tattoos on his legs—she admires.

Sometimes I hide behind Colleen. She pats my arm and apologizes to guests when I forget towels behind the door. If I have a slow morning, she extends sympathy. She sticks up for me against the huffy front desk workers. I know she is on my team.

Sometimes I try to hide behind my uniform. Crossing the parking lot to the employee dining room for a lunch break, I weave through crowds of tourists meandering toward Old Faithful's boardwalk. I don't want to answer questions about forest fire damage or the geyser's next eruption, but tourists interpret my uniform as a sign of expertise and servitude. Room attendants usually deal with the gawking public indirectly, not head on, like tour guides or restaurant waitstaff. Guests rarely approach me with their gripes. Once while I was dragging my cart between cabins, a man wearing yellow-tinted glasses accosted me, fuming that his room wasn't ready and that he and his wife couldn't take hot showers after riding all day on their motorcycle. I shrugged, showed him my list, told him he'd have to duke it out with the front desk. I wondered what action he'd hoped for from a lowly room attendant. There's freedom in having so little power.

In the employee caste system, my uniform marks me as a drone. The restaurant waitstaff's snappy tuxedo shirts, the gift-shop employees' three-piece suits, the dining room workers' checked pants and puffy chef hats clearly outclass me. But my uniform elicits sympathetic nods from folks who've climbed out of housekeeping into other jobs. On lunch breaks in the employee dining room, I sit at a long table surrounded by other weary room attendants. We trade stories from the trenches. An eavesdropping, middle-management type might write us off as a bunch of sickos, but I have no problem downing mashed potatoes and green beans while listening to stories of vomit in bathtubs or misplaced dirty diapers or prolific pubes in a bathtub drain.

By the time I clock out, I yearn for a hot shower and a cold soda. The uniform gets crumpled in a pile of laundry at the foot of my bed. I wear civilian clothes to dinner and blend in with the geyser-watching masses. Like an undercover cop, I am stealthy; only the espresso-cart woman and the gift-shop clerks—who've seen me in the employee dining room—know my secret identity.

My work here is not for an audience. If a family of five is making trips from their minivan to their cabin for cameras and raincoats and last-minute potty breaks, I cannot, in good conscience, spread clean rags on the bed or roll out the scrubbed shower mat to pick out the hairs wrapped tightly around its suction cups. They should not see my rubber-gloved hands— the same hands that have cleaned ten different toilets that day—nearly graze their lineup of toothbrushes in an attempt to remove milky-white spots from the mirror.

Once a chatty retired couple from California left four fruit bars splayed like a decorative fan on the low dresser as a sort of tip; perhaps they felt a vague obligation, since they'd returned to their cabin the afternoon before while I was scrubbing the bathtub. A great housekeeping paradox: If guests come in while I'm cleaning, I feel like I've been caught doing something dirty. I don't like surprises.

At each door I'm supposed to knock and announce "housekeeping" in a polite singsong three distinct times before I use my master key. My coworker JoJo runs through his three warnings in a rapid monotone. He also wears Velcro tennis shoes I associate with grandpas and deems anything that's remarkable, good or bad, as "ghostly." He wants to marry his Snow Lodge sweetheart at the employee pub. I feel silly announcing my presence three times, but I have to give guests the heads-up. I only stumble upon an occasional heavy sleeper—nothing particularly racy.

My work demands invisibility. A table free from sticky orange-juice rings, a lineup of clean washcloths folded into thirds like business letters: these call no attention to themselves. My work succeeds by what is not seen (brittle pine needles in the carpet, grimy shadows around the bathtub, fine gray dust on the heating unit). My work wipes out what others create: a mess. But every guest is entitled to a clean room to start with. My work succeeds if, as my boss, Cynthia, says, each guest can maintain the illusion that they are the first people to ever stay in their room. It is best if I leave no trace.

When I first arrived in Wyoming, I told a Snake River guide I was headed for Yellowstone. She asked if I knew I was moving atop a volcano. A molten magma chamber simmers beneath the park, fueling the geothermal features—hot springs, muddy paint pots, geysers—clustered there. Signs warn us to stay on marked paths and boardwalks, because the crust of earth can thin unexpectedly over thermals. On hikes, I spy traces of a bison carcass slumped by a geyser or spring. Animals can't read, the rangers quip. I cringe, imagining a careless bison plunking into the mouth of a boiling pool, swallowed by the flower of its blue-green heat.

Besides the heat pulsing underground, fire leaves its mark above ground too. Charred trees stand like gravestones as one enters the park. I have only vague memories of newscasts about the sweeping fires of 1988. When I arrived in Yellowstone, I was ill prepared for the devastation. Rangers explain that they tried to snuff out manmade fires, but those sparked by nature were mostly left to run their course. Rangers had to stand by and watch grandeur destroy itself.

Cynthia manages the Old Faithful Snow Lodge Housekeeping Department. Her roots burrow in the Midwest, but she's lived in Yellowstone for the last ten years. Cynthia wears glasses, no makeup, and a trucker-style ball cap. The construction-paper sign on her office door lists all the places where she might be: at home, at lunch, in a meeting, out at the cabins, an unspecified "Other." She is punctilious about the sign; the pushpin follows her every move.

Cynthia has dissected housekeeping into minute parts. She has timed herself making beds and will reveal her personal best, but not in a bragging way. Her inspections create mild panic, because she demands we clean each bathroom by the book: scrubbing, rinsing, drying every crevice. She caresses a shower wall; she can read it like Braille and knows whether I've used the proper "scrub-free" cleanser or tried to trick her with glass cleaner.

Cynthia says my race is against my watch. I wear my watch every day and glance at it several times in each room; it's comforting to know time has not stood motionless while I've been scouring and folding. Although room cleaning becomes more and more involuntary, my routine is not streamlined. I only speed up if I find a freebie; I say kind things under my breath about the chummy guests who leave one of the room's double beds untouched or the tourists who ignore the showers.

I cried after Cynthia and I inspected one of my rooms together. I mean, I nodded in assent while she pointed out wrinkled beds and a dirty ice bucket. But when Cynthia turned the spare roll of toilet paper so that its seam faced the wall, I knew I could never please her. The "guest side" is all-important, she reminded me; the closest bed corner, the hand towels with dangling tags, the arrangement of hand soap in the doily-lined basket, anything the guest sees at first glance—these demand attention. These details slow me down, but I'd rather deal with them myself than have to redo a room.

I resent the hold Cynthia has on me. Were she a tyrant, I could fling imaginary darts at her while dusting cobwebs out of windows. But Cynthia is nothing if not professional and awkwardly genial. And although my time doesn't improve much over the summer, she notes my thoroughness and attention to detail. I savor her compliments. She praises my bathtubs in particular, their smooth texture and hairlessness. This is our bond—Cynthia confides in me that she excels at bathrooms too.

On my last day in the park, I'm not scheduled to work, but I end up helping Pamela finish her long list of rooms. I've already turned in my uniform, and I feel much less official cleaning rooms in jeans and a T-shirt. I expected to clean my last rooms with perverse nostalgia, an acute awareness that these would be the last beds I'd make, or the last towels I'd fold, in Yellowstone. But these are just more rooms. When I turn in my paperwork, my offer of a handshake becomes a brisk, unforeseen hug from Cynthia.

Some of the earliest explorers in Yellowstone returned to the industrial east with sketches and tales of their trek. Almost no one believed them, until more surveyors marked out what became the first national park in 1872. But borders aren't usually solid lines—except on a map. Nature is fluid. Bison and wolves, river and wind obey no constraints and mingle outside this sanctuary. I too pass surreptitiously in and out of the park, by ranger stations and blackened, forlorn tree trunks. But those lodgepole pine have seeds that fire releases, the rangers say. See those stubby green seedlings growing beside their blackened parents? Come back in a hundred years, and you'll never know what happened.

No Turning Back

Christa Sadler

The roar grew louder. It sounded like a jet plane about to leave the runway. As we rounded the corner, I could tell where the roar was coming from, but I couldn't see a thing. The river dropped off in a straight horizon.

The rapids I knew on the rivers of Oregon and Northern California fell away in nice, long ramps of whitewater, and they sounded like applause. But this rapid had a deep growl to it, a basso born of more rushing water than any five of the rivers I knew combined.

Both my guidebook and the trainer in my boat said this was Badger Creek Rapid, Mile 8 on the Colorado River through the Grand Canyon. "Just follow the boats in front of you," Dave explained calmly. "It's fun." I suppose if he had known my real level of experience, he might not have been so calm. This was the first time I was rowing my own boat down the Colorado River. At times I couldn't even imagine surviving the trip, much less wanting to come back to do it over and over again—every summer, every year—until I could no longer hold a pair of oars.

A few years before, I traveled as a commercial passenger on a motor rig in the Grand Canyon. For six glorious days on very high water, we rarely used the motor; we simply floated and watched. I was like a kid in a candy store. I had just begun to study geology and was acting as "trip geologist" for a group of friends. Hour by hour, we sat on the front of the boat and examined our geology guides, then compared what we were reading to what we were seeing. I was in heaven, and on about Day 4, I remember someone saying to me, "Christa, you look like you belong here."

Whoever that was—bless his heart—was right. Although three years later, listening to that awful roar at the top of Badger Creek Rapid, I wasn't so sure.

"I don't think I should do this, Dave. Maybe you should take the oars."

"Bullshit! Just follow the other boats."

After that interminable slowness at the top of the rapid, the current was finally speeding up; there was no turning back. To this day, that feeling of gliding faster and faster down that silky smooth tongue of water makes my heart quicken and brings a smile to my face.

As we dropped over the edge, we faced an absolute chaos of whitewater. I had learned to head the boat straight into the waves, but how could I do that when waves appeared on all sides at once? I developed tunnel vision; there was no world but the one right in front of my boat. Both oars were ripped out of my hands, and I slid halfway off my seat as a wave slapped me in the face. I couldn't pick out any features of the rapid; it was sheer confusion.

When I noticed the waves getting smaller and more regular, I scrambled for the oars. The boat was full of water and heavy as a cement truck as we wallowed out into the calm pool at the base of the rapid. We were through, although I was pretty sure I had nothing to do with it. Dave was grinning. "Welcome to the Grand Canyon, Christa! This is a great river. The rapids start out easy and get harder, so you can learn as you go along."

Harder?

The days and nights of my first motor trip as a passenger have extended into a colorful blur, but I have one clear memory from that journey—the incident that changed my life. We had reached the Little Colorado, where the water was backed up into a vivid turquoise swimming pool into which we fell, delighted, to play for hours. A small, orange raft bearing four passengers and a tan, muscular boatwoman came down the Little Colorado toward us. We stopped to watch them pass. They all waved and then headed on out into the green Colorado. The boatwoman looked so competent, so healthy, so *right*. I remember thinking, *I want to belong here like that woman.*

After the trip, I went straight back to California and applied for rowing positions. I joined up with a small company in Oregon that offered a four-day training trip on the Rogue River. Throughout the trip, people talked about which rivers to run, and I would say, "I want to run the Grand Canyon."

"There are lots of harder rivers," people countered. *That's okay*, I would think. *I just want to run the Grand Canyon.* I couldn't explain why.

I was hired as a guide on the Rogue, the Deschutes, and the Upper and Lower Klamath. I spent the summer learning the difference between a hole and a lateral wave, how to ferry upstream to slow down and get across the current, how to tuck behind rocks, how to tie knots and rig a boat. When I applied for positions rowing baggage boats on the Colorado, I was pretty sure I could handle it. I couldn't have been more mistaken.

That first boat on the Colorado was a slug, with a low bow and stern specifically designed to scoop in water as you went through the smallest waves. I was used to fourteen-foot boats loaded for four days; this eighteen-foot raft was loaded for thirteen days. I was used to eight-foot matchstick oars; these were eleven-foot telephone poles. I was used to slow-moving water that allowed you time to maneuver and correct errors; this fast, powerful water allowed no room for mistakes. And worst of all, I had rowed only with pinned oars, where the oar blade is held permanently at right angles to the water. This boat had open oarlocks, and the oars could rotate at will.

Three rapids into the trip, at House Rock, I discovered the frustration of open oarlocks. I needed to make a move that was new for me: a downstream ferry. It is particularly critical at House Rock, because if you follow the current, you end up in a boat-eater of a hole. I was poised, ready to take that first powerful stroke. Unbeknownst to me, my oar blade had turned parallel to the surface; as I pulled back with all my strength, my oar sliced cleanly through the water and I almost flew backward off my seat before I regained control. By that time of course, it was too late, the move had been missed, and we ended up squarely in the washing machine of the hole. Luckily, I was only rowing the gear boat.

I was learning, quickly.

I never did flip, but I am not sure why. I certainly should have, given some of my runs. Mr. Toad's Wild Ride: oars gone, feet in the air, backward, sideways, hitting rocks, completely out of control. At Horn Creek—notoriously difficult in low water—I missed the "right" move and went backward, straight into the jaws of the beast, hit the rock wall sideways, almost flipped, broke a spare oar, and washed my trainer out of the front of the boat. As he climbed, sputtering, into the back of the boat, he struck me as looking a little bedraggled. No wonder.

On the motor trip three years earlier, I met a fellow passenger, an artist who talked about what he saw in the canyon walls. He took pictures all the way down the river—not of vistas, or ruins, or waterfalls, but of textures and shadows and shapes. When he got these home, he said, he would paint them.

Looking at the place in this new light, I began to see that the canyon offers much more than just rapids and beautiful side hikes. I would watch Jim sitting quietly beside a wall, examining it, and go find my own wall or pile of stones to examine. It is easy to see the canyon for its obvious grandness; I was learning to see the subtleties. Slowly the unfamiliar rocks transcended the boundaries of names. Kaibab, Coconino, Supai, and Tapeats entered my mind as textures and colors and shapes, not just geological formations. I began to notice the way the sunlight moved down the wall in a widening golden band in the morning, and back up again in the afternoon, until it was just a narrow bronze sliver at the top. I saw how the calm water looked like polished steel in the early morning, and how the rapids looked like a million horses galloping if you watched them for a while.

But at the oars of my own boat for the first time in the canyon, I wasn't looking around. All the geology I had learned departed my head to make space for anxiety. My world became a narrow path of rushing water, bounded by inescapable walls.

Then one morning, after we had come through a series of rapids and the water would be calm for a while, I woke up before sunrise, relaxed for the first time in days. I lay on my boat and listened to the water gurgling by as I watched the sky lighten by degrees—first dove gray, then pale lilac, finally silver blue with a touch of yellow in the eastern sky. A canyon wren trilled its descending call, and one of the passengers chuckled softly. I looked up at the walls. Suddenly, instead of confining, their solidity felt like arms welcoming me home. The afternoon before, when I had come through one rapid in good style, with a smile on my face, Dave had slapped me on the back and said, "*That's* what you're here for!" Now, as I lay watching dawn come to the canyon, I thought, *No*, this *is what I'm here for*. Something had changed. I felt like I belonged.

Still, Lava Falls was ahead. Most of the way downriver, I had been worrying about the falls. I remembered them from my first trip as a passenger. That time, our boatmen thought it wisest to take the run down the left side, and I barely got wet. To tell you the truth, I had been disappointed, as I now understand passengers often are if they don't get "the big ride." But we had watched the third boat of our party run down the right. Their 33-foot boat hit the second wave and almost disappeared. Then they hit the big wave at the bottom and completely disappeared. All I could see was the baseball cap of the guide standing in the motor well. When they emerged from the bottom and motored over to join us, the people on the boat were drenched and ecstatic. For the first time, I understood the euphoria and the camaraderie that comes with a successful run through a big rapid.

Now I was getting ready to row my own boat through Lava Falls. We stood at the scout above the rapid, and what I saw I could only describe as chaos. The only thing I could pick out of the mess was a huge waterfall called the Ledge. It looked like most of the river's flow went into its yawning, cavernous hole. That thing could swallow a Greyhound bus without a belch, and if someone went in, it seemed to me that the boat would stay stuck for a long, long time. The boatmen explained the run to me, and we started back to the boats. I felt sick.

Then Ed turned around and yelled, "Just watch out at the top, because the river is going to do something you don't expect, okay?"

What?! What was the river going to do? But he was off on his own boat, getting ready. We pulled out into that slow, slow, interminably slow current.

Dave was in the front, ready to be weight into the waves if it was needed. We were sideways to the current, so that I could adjust my positioning before turning straight downstream. Somewhere out there to the left was the Ledge Hole, the one place in the whole rapid I knew I didn't want to go. In front of me, the world dropped off into noise. Suddenly the current began to sweep left, fast. I had no idea where I was, but I knew I didn't want to go into the Hole sideways, so I spun the stern downstream and pulled hard. I ran the rapid dead backward.

When we reached the bottom, brim-full of water and oarless, Dave screamed, "What was *that?!* Don't ever do that again!" Scared and shaking, I steadfastly maintained that I had done the right thing to avoid going into the Ledge sideways. Turns out we were nowhere near it; the current always sweeps a little left before going back to the right. You just have to wait it out.

I still think Ed could have explained that a little better.

As we approached the end of our motor trip that first time on the river, my friends excitedly discussed the upcoming helicopter flight and the hot shower waiting at the rim. But all I could think about was the fact that I was leaving. My eyes had been opened to a place and a life that I could never have invented in my wildest fantasies. I'd slept under a sky that defied imagination; I'd watched lightning bolts shatter the gray clouds during a summer thunderstorm. I'd learned more geology in six days than in any semester in a classroom. The river had flowed through all of this like a binding thread, an ever-present teacher. My only thoughts were of returning one day, and I couldn't stop crying. Two ravens had danced overhead, calling, daring me to come back.

When we reached Diamond Creek early on the 13th morning of my first rowing trip, I saw the place was scarred by years of derigging and takeout vehicles. It contrasted sharply with the nearly pristine beaches we had slept on for the past 12 nights. Looking at it, I started to cry. We pulled in, and I began to take apart my boat, still crying. The same feeling I'd had three years before swept over me: *I don't want to leave.* The other boatmen stared at me curiously. *Too much stress,* they reasoned. I heard a raucous cry from overhead and looked up to see two ravens circling, reminding me that they'd be here when I returned. I smiled and walked toward the truck. Behind me, the river flowed on around a bend, out of sight, no turning back.

Hunkered at the Gateway

Christine Byl

They call us seasonals. People who move to a park for a job with the park—me, 15 years ago to Glacier National Park, in Western Montana, as a laborer on a trail crew. In northern parks like Glacier, May and October are the shoulders of summer, and they stretch a six-month work season between them. But after the ground freezes and the tourists leave, most seasonals follow. Travel and ski bumming, winter jobs, another semester of school. Back home to the family ranch. A stint at the South Pole. The reasons vary, but the outcome is the same: Seasonals leave.

Until, sometimes, we stay. Laborers become crew leaders, returning to a job for years and years. Some get promoted to a term job—or a permanent one even, with health care and retirement: a career, that weighty word. Or we fall in love with the place and can't see leaving once the work season's over. We rent or build houses nearby. We buy a horse or have kids or get a dog team, hitching ourselves to a post that's anchored deeper than just "park" or "job."

By the time we stayed put, my husband, Gabe, and I had worked trails for ten seasons in three different places, moving every six months. Seven seasons in Glacier. One for the Forest Service in Cordova, when we moved to Alaska. And then again for the National Park Service, in Denali, where despite our years of trail work experience, we started from scratch: seasonals,

167

somewhere new. Our first two seasons in Denali were broken up by winters in Anchorage, where I was in graduate school. But after our second summer in the park, we had no reason to leave when the trails season finished. Degree in hand, no home elsewhere, no desire to move. October came. Summer people left. We stayed.

I was still seasonal, on paper at least. To the park, I was a temporary employee, a trail crew leader who was laid off when gloves wore out and the snow flew. But staying felt different. For the first time in our twelve-year history together, Gabe and I let six months pass without moving. No sorting our possessions, no protracted goodbyes, no switched-over utilities. No identity based on being about-to-leave. The realization was as striking as sun in my eyes: I lived in Denali. Five years after that first choice to stay, I now know all four seasons of the year here, back-to-back, year to year. Permanent. For now.

My first summer in Denali, Gabe and I lived in C-Camp, the Park Service's seasonal housing compound just inside the park entrance. Brown cabins lined the road to the maintenance lot, where out-of-state Subarus plastered with bumper stickers sat parked next to ten-yard dump trucks with Peterbilt mud flaps. We walked to the trails shop from our one-room log A-frame, its rent invisible, taken directly out of our paychecks like chits at the company store. We showered in the public washhouse, and on weekends off, planned trips into Denali's backcountry. My reality was defined by the park, the job, the parameters of a transplant up for the summer. I knew only a few folks who lived in the nearby town of Healy—the trails foreman, in Denali ten years; a fellow trail-crew leader, born in Alaska; and a handful of permanents from other divisions.

Returning the second summer to Denali, Gabe and I moved out of C-Camp. We wanted privacy, a place we could have a dog, neighbors, a life beyond the park and its rhythms. We moved north, as was our bent, outside Healy, whose population, according to the 2000 census, was 984. Healy's year-round employers are the coal mine, visible across the Nenana River; the power plant (coal-fired); and the park, "protected" from both of them, 12 miles to the south. The two-lane Parks Highway passes through the middle of Healy, and its face to the world is the quintessential small-town one—two gas stations, a ratty bar, a truck-stop diner with the usual gut-bomb breakfasts served all day. Off the road is a K–12 school whose small library is open to the public four afternoons a week, a community center with a tiny clinic, and a volunteer fire department. Healy booms when summer tourists flock to Denali, but people pass through quickly. Despite its scenic backdrop, Healy is as invisible to travelers as the apartment buildings outside a New York City subway car, or the neat ranch houses off Interstate 90.

Beyond the highway artery, residents cluster up ridges and down creeks, tucked into aspen groves, hidden in brush. We live up Panguingue Creek—"out Stampede," in the local parlance. Stampede Road tees west off the highway toward the park on the skyline, turning from pavement to gravel to two-track to trail, and finally passable only by mountain bike and ATV—or in winter, by dog teams and snow-gos. Out Stampede there are a few big houses, but most people live in modest homes and tiny cabins they've built out-of-pocket. A tarp-covered lumber pile and a yard full of sled dogs are far more common than a heated garage.

Our first rental was particularly rustic (a 16-by-20 log cabin with no running water), but by no means unusual. Septic systems and wells indicate a resident's longevity—or at least permanent job money socked away or borrowed to get 300 feet below ground, where the water table lies. The rest of us shit in outhouses and collect rainwater in 50-gallon barrels and haul drinking water from the well house with five-gallon jugs or PVC tanks in the back of pickup trucks. Friends with showers offer them freely. At dry-cabin potlucks, people bring their own full water bottles, so as not to burden the hosts with more hauling.

Healy is in some ways a town all its own, a place like nowhere else I've been, where the post office bulletin board boasts lynx hides for sale (by a local fourth-grader with a trap line), and the air smells like coal dust and tundra plants mixed by a muscular wind. In other ways, it's Interior Alaska's version of the same old town you pass through on the way to any park, both entry and buffer. However common, or however special, Healy is the odd little place I've called home. It's a place made up of, among all the other things, seasons.

In winter, Healy hunkers down. On the solstice, there are about four hours of light, and chances are it's cold. Life gets stripped down. The nearest town of any size is Fairbanks—two hours north by a snow-packed, two-lane highway—and we go on daylong sojourns for groceries, dog food, building materials, bookstore and doctor visits, a movie or Thai food if there's time. Other than those biweekly town trips, we're on our own. Healy has a little store where you can get a rock-hard or a past-gone avocado, chips at $6.50 a bag, or a gallon of milk for the same. But there's no "stocking up" in Healy. In winter, you get what you get.

Don't come to Healy looking for a chai. This is not *Outside* magazine's Best Town in America. No university town accoutrements, no ski resort nearby, no yoga studio with bamboo radiant floors. And though I've used—and often miss—that cultural tackle, Healy has the charm that comes from its lack of artifice, the old kind of dorkiness—uncalculated. An informal tai chi group meets on Thursday nights in the school gym. No harp music or fancy workout clothes; we bend and bow in baggy long underwear to the tinny commands of a Chinese woman on a warped VHS tape. Here, *chi* smells more like sweaty socks than incense.

Like any small town, Healy has entrenched divisions—pro-road, anti-mine, more wilderness, no zoning. Yet, nothing's simple: Park employees have trap lines, and coal miners have dog teams. We all complain about the price of gas, and about the tourists who flock to see "the bus" 20 miles out Stampede. (Thank you, Jon Krakauer and Sean Penn.) Healy is a tiny and pragmatic place, invisible to anyone who doesn't live here, and that's what bonds those of us who do. There are ideological divisions and old grudges, to be sure. But animosities have to sit alongside what we have in common: remoteness, self-reliance, weather that matters. Undiluted by a larger population, we're really neighbors. During a deep freeze, everyone clumps around in the same insulated bibs and Bunny boots, politics concealed beneath the veneer of the practical. (Except for the teenagers, who slip from truck cab to high school clad in the same flip-flops and soccer shorts they wear in July.)

Solitary tasks make up the winter days of many residents—hauling water, running the dogs, caring for the baby, drywalling the basement. To ward off too much loneliness, locals gather for any reason we can muster. There are book clubs, knitting groups, poker nights, hockey games, school pageants, a periodic slide show by someone back from exotic travels. Also, gatherings at the community center: a chili feed, a Borough hearing, and midwinter, the holiday extravaganza—Healy on Ice, where Santa rides a Zamboni at the outdoor rink behind the school.

Don't let this list fool you. Healy is quiet. Some days, when the cabin feels dark and small, and there's no way to stay warm outside for longer than an hour, I wish for a clean, well-lighted space, a magazine, and a hot drink amid the bustle of the public sphere, the haven of anonymity. Not here. There's no hot, no bustle, no public. No anonymous.

Up here, winter makes you local. Denali as workplace means summer months on the trails, tools in hand, always on the move, crowds of seasonals gathered at bars and parties and river-access pullouts. In summer, it's clear why anyone's here—the job is full-time, the schedule packed, the world hospitable. But while summer makes this an easier place to live, the other three seasons make this home.

When Gabe and I chose to stay past the usual cusp, the reason wasn't the weather or the job or the potlucks. We stayed because it's where our life was. Now, with each exodus of summer's ease, we settle in with canned goods and Netflix and our ski loop behind the cabin, where the snow blows into drifts as hard as tarmac, and we never see anyone.

Spring in Denali tugs at late-March days, when a long sun softens snow, and warmer winds blow in possibilities. But March often brings the year's coldest snap—winter reminding us she still has the reins. Only in late April, as southern climates watch for crocuses, do we see the beginning of the end of ice. Alaska's fifth season, squeezed between winter and spring, is "break-up": break-up of rivers, as shed-sized chunks of ice give way; break-up of frozen driveways and roads, thaw triggering spring's buckle-and-heave, so the same potholes open up and gravel roads ripple with washboard; break-up of overflow, the layers of water and ice that percolate frozen-solid creeks and rivers; and break-up of snowpack in the tundra lowlands, exposing winter-kill and last year's cranberries. It's fitting that break-up's label alludes to the end of romance: grim, gray, trudging. While it's happening, it seems it will never pass. It always does.

Look quick to catch spring. April's ice overlaps May's buds. Aspens go from hint of pale green to fully leafed out in three days. Spring blooms thrust through snow, and bushes that will yield berries by August have tiny flowers while ice lingers in creek bottoms. Spring's window is short—just time enough to get its business done, jump-starting life, issuing in the fervent days of June, only three months before the freeze takes hold again. Blown kiss, curt bow, spring exits the stage quick: Summer waits in the wings, ready to pass in a panic, looking over its shoulder, winter's breath already on its neck.

Summer in Denali is fast and furious, a drunk on a spree before he quits for good, a kid out past bedtime in beckoning light. Mid-April, it sets in that winter is on the wane, and then *boom*, the upward climb toward solstice, June 21, the longest day, when nightfall is just a fleeting, thicker dusk. The mountains thaw, the rivers burgeon, and tourism rages by June. Hotels and shops throw off window boards, winter's toothy bite a secret most summer folks will never guess. RVs and bus tours flood the highways. Elderly folks clutch each other's arms in crosswalks. Newlyweds buy cheap T-shirts, snap photos near anything that says "Alaska."

At work, we get serious. Denali-the-place is open all winter, but in May, Denali-the-park rouses from its six-month slow season. Employees show up again, as sure as bears coming out of their dens. In the trails shop, one week there's the indoor organizing and training, the buttoning up of winter's projects (notching logs, fixing tools), and the next week, the full-throated roar of construction time. The ground thaws day by inch, and we move dirt with Bobcats and shovels and backs, applying ourselves to trail work in a fury that's adrenalized by the ticking clock. Bridges, switchbacks, survey, rock work: There won't be time for all we have to do.

Outside of work, summer to-do lists are just as epic—building projects, fishing trip to fill the freezer for the year, peaks to climb, gardens growing, visitors coming, going, coming. Weeks pass, blurred. Days go by with four hours sleep until I collapse for a weekend of deep breaths, wonder how long this pace can go on even as I pull the light in close, rub it into my skin, save it up against the craving dark. After June's longest day, we're over the apex and dropping toward the bottom of the bell curve. First it's slow—July loiters, some years warm and dry, others rainy and cool—but August hits, and even when it's warm, the light is leaving. Berries ripen overnight. Tourists lessen, trickle, then stop, as if their source dried up. Wolves and bears scarf all the calories they can find, and snowshoe hares and ptarmigan change to the white that will conceal them through the winter.

In Denali, summer is the intermission to winter's concert. We guzzle drinks in the lobby with friends, buy CDs, and make a quick trip to the bathroom, aware that at any minute, the lights will flicker, and the rest of the show will begin.

Healy Index

Pairs of shorts I own: 3

Pairs of boots I own (including ski boots): 20

Households we know with between 1 and 20 sled dogs: 13

Lowest temperature I've felt in the Interior: −68°F

Highest temperature I've felt in the Interior: 91°F

Minimum time to plug in engine block before starting truck at 20 below: 2 hours

Gallons of berries harvested in an average summer: 6

Copper River sockeye salmon per household allowed on a dip-netting permit: 30

Number of pint jars it takes to can a single salmon: 4

Miles per hour you can ski at 20 below: 3

Miles per hour you can skijor at 20 below: 6

Maximum price for a gallon of unleaded gas in 2008: $5.11

Number of creeks or rivers the highway crosses between Healy and the park: 7

Closest proximity of a moose to our cabin wall: 2 inches
Most caribou seen on an afternoon ski: 30
Months in the year with wolf scat on the back trail: 12
Number of friends with a heated garage: 2

Autumn in Denali seduces me every year, when nature reinvents shade, palette, tone. People think of New England for colors, and the Midwest, or small towns in mountain states, full of maples and oaks that transplants brought from back east to line the boulevards of their adopted homes. No one thinks of Denali.

When I rave about fall, my sister says, "I thought you didn't have trees." But color doesn't need trees. Fall colors the north not in canopies above our heads but on the ground, chemistry's carpet unfurling underfoot. Reddened willows, lichen's green glow, squashy mushrooms in earthen tones. Berries—snow, cran, blue, cloud, nagoon, bear, salmon—in orange, white, wine, and almost black. Aspens draw the eye up with their taffeta glimmer and lisp, but in autumn's conversation, the ground has the floor.

I am an existentialist at heart, and I love fall in part for its contemplative underpinnings, the way it makes me notice the concrete world (everything's dying) and think about the abstract one (everything dies). When the trees and brush go aflame right before the leaves and blooms pale at winter, I also wonder: Will I have even *minutes* as full of purpose as these plants do, when my very hue is tinted by the tasks to which I've turned my hands?

Sixty-three degrees north, winter takes up half the year, so it gets another mention before my year's end. Mid-October through mid-April is cold, snow early on the ground or windy and bare straight through Christmas. Midwinter brings long snaps at 40 below (shorter than decades ago, the old-timers say), and if the mercury rises past 20, it's just as likely to rocket up to 40 for a fluky Chinook, the warm and blowsy front that tears through a few times a year, carrying with it smells of other seasons, other worlds.

Winter's rhythms are made up of wake and sleep, motion and stillness, the race against the clock (finish chores, go for ski), and the hours of reading in lacy-windowed cabins warmed by fuel oil's glow. In winter's crisp nights, I stumble to the outhouse: an impossibility of light. Nights black as a blanket over the head are backdrop for the aurora, that scientific borealis acid trip. I know about solar winds and charged particles circling the magnetic poles, but the first time I saw a pink and green display, I thought *birthday party*. On a cold night, a deep breath—even through a face mask and the zipped neck of your puffiest coat—burns the throat, but you have to be outside. Watching the aurora from indoors isn't the same. Under that sky, it's clear how fully *in* this universe we are, as the roof of our home lifts and swirls.

In every season, we contend with light and dark. Outsiders ask how we stand the dark, but the light is harder for me. Summer's long days are intoxicating—roof the shed at midnight! start a climb at four in the morning!—but it's also exhausting, the never stopping, the sense that all things are possible, all the time. In summer, I crave dark, cold, snow. Dark is less expectant than light. It shuts out all stimuli but what you choose for yourself. Dark gives permission for mulling, for hours of reading and late breakfasts and the free-of-sensory-overload unconscious time that rebuilds me. Dark is an ally.

Dark is also an adversary. Some begin to lament the growing dark in September and soldier on until spring with a kind of bitter resolve that connotes pioneers in sod houses. Everyone has a tip for thriving in the dark months—buy a SAD light, dump that needy boyfriend, take up knitting. The key for me in learning to love the Interior winter was simple: Move vigorously outside for at least an hour, and expand my sense of day. In summer we sleep when it's light out, and in winter, dark needn't mean quit. A full moon lights a night skijor, reflected starlight on snow a rural streetlamp. Winter evenings mean lit candles in the windows, a dim log cabin the excuse to let Christmas lights glow for months. Winter tells me, push past the limits the body's clock sets for itself. Expect darkness. Watch for light.

Dark can be inconvenient. I hate quitting a task because of a forgotten headlamp or a waning moon, hate banging my shin on the porch step because it's too black to see. There's pressure in winter daylight, time slipped through fingers: At two o'clock you begin to think about dinner, at seven, bed. If you're sad or overwhelmed, dark seems bottomless, a soul-plummet in the worst kind of freefall.

But dark is also magical. Winter feeds a primordial hunger, an urge to curl up and lick your paws, to pause on the questions that light rushes us past. I take my cues from our two old sled dogs, who sleep soundest in winter, curled up in a pocket they've melted in the snow, or so near the woodstove their coats are hot to touch. Deep winter is the cave of the year.

Sanity hangs in the balance of light and dark. A year in the Interior is like a day anywhere else; it takes the whole spectrum for it to make sense. Together, the seasons have symmetry, the calendar folded on itself like a paper snowflake. Now that I am home here, it's hard to imagine anything less extreme. My body has been calibrated toward the 12-month cycle, and now I can sleep with sun on my face in June and wake (groggily) at six in the morning in December, ready to begin my day in a day that has not yet begun.

No matter what the season, in a house with no plumbing, we imitate the pleasures of civilized life. Our bathroom is an outhouse, which contrary to expectation is a wonderful thing.

A bathroom in the yard puts you out in the world first thing in the morning, no matter what the weather. In winter, a piece of closed-cell blue foam insulation, cut to fit over the hole, makes a fine seat, as warm as anyone's indoor throne.

For a sink, drop a stainless-steel basin into the counter, no fixtures necessary. Drain it with an open-ended pipe, five-gallon bucket poised beneath. Haul water from the well in plastic cubies; in summer, supplement it with the 40-gallon barrel that sits beneath a gutter downspout. Use the water (so icy cold out of the well all year long it hurts your teeth) to fill the Gatorade jug that poses as a faucet on the sink's edge, press the little spigot: running water. For washing your face or the dishes, heat up water in the kettle or the big tin pans. Once used to it, you can almost forget this isn't how everyone lives. The plates are clean. The chicken soup is made with rainwater. Paper towels are a guilty luxury. You pretend you're normal until the day you forget to empty the slop bucket, and you drain a can of beans or dump a soaking pan, and that last drop brings the water over the bucket's top, flooding, thick and stinky, onto the floor, the rug, your feet. It doesn't matter then if it's warm out or cold, light or dark. There's only one way to vent the disgust, and that is to yell at the top of your lungs the refrain favored by inhabitants of dry cabins all over the state, the admission to the plumbed universe that we're posers at best: *My sink drains into a fucking bucket!*

Seasons upon seasons past the day we moved to the Denali region, Gabe and I don't work for the Park Service anymore. Despite its reputation as "America's Best Idea," the Park Service has a dark side, and it was high time for us to shake off the petty management dramas, the grueling bureaucracy, the taking for granted. Often, especially for seasonals, leaving a job means leaving a place. But Denali doesn't belong to me via the Park

Service anymore. I belong to the place, via the claim made by time spent and things learned. Over the past few years, figuring out a way to stay, we've bought a small chunk of land, built a little studio on it, put up a yurt, and started our own trails business. We travel a lot for work, and between the busy field season and wintertime forays, I feel less nested than when we worked for the Park Service. We don't spend every month here, and our cadence feels syncopated, our weight shifting. Still, Healy remains my mental home, the place I think of when I'm anywhere else. The park, that old ground zero, feels like a different world.

We do end up in C-Camp once in a while, for dinner with friends who still live there, or to poach a shower after a backcountry trip. When I drive through, past the cabin we lived in, I remember that first summer fondly—our introduction to a landscape, the edge of community, by way of a park entrance. There's a new swath cut through C-Camp now, a wider-than-it-needed-to-be road corridor leading to a bigger parking lot, better maintenance buildings, a new trails shop for a bigger crew. The crew leaders now are the folks we trained back when we were the new guys. Our big projects are ancient history, our mark there all but forgotten. Nothing stays the same. The old days always seem like the good ones. From far off, it's easy to mistake rust for gold.

If I've learned anything during the time that I've been a seasonal, it's that to know a place is a tough and complicated goal. It means far more than knowing all the hiking trails or where to get a cheap beer—the easy discoveries anywhere new, what transplants learn first. Knowing a place means knowing its seasons, and what indicates them: when the Sandhill cranes pass over on their way from the Arctic to the equator, when the cranberries are ripe, which two weeks the wood frogs sing loud. Knowing when to put out the rainwater barrel, because a hard freeze is unlikely, and when to harvest carrots, because a hard freeze could come at any time.

Knowing a place means investing in it like you don't plan to go anywhere, even if you might. For me that's meant volunteering at the library, searching for the owner of a lost dog, going to community meetings, especially when they make my blood boil. Knowing a place means knowing what I love (the smell of tundra plants in rain), what I hate (small-town gossip), and what has nothing at all to do with me (when the bears den up). Mostly, it means tuning into a place beyond just what it can offer. This takes daily effort, daily noticing. Annie Dillard says that "how we spend our days is, of course, how we spend our lives," and that's exactly why a seasonal life can also be a permanent one.

Looking back over the fifteen years since I first showed up in a trails shop with new Carhartts and soft hands, I can see all those days stacked up, built into months, then years. And now, here it is, a hunch that was growing in me all along, from Missoula, Glacier, Anchorage, Cordova, Denali, and on: Living somewhere doesn't mean you know it, and a job alone doesn't make a place a home. It takes work to do that.

Venus at Minus 50

Tom Walker

Home, on the boundary of Denali National Park and Preserve, Alaska.

This morning it is 42 degrees below zero. To be more precise, it is −42 degrees Fahrenheit, which equals −41 degrees Celsius. If it is this cold here, down in the canyon it must be even colder.

The first thing I do after getting up is feed the stove. Despite generous and frequent meals of spruce and birch, it has been ravenous for two weeks now. "The Resolute," as the manufacturer calls it, has done an admirable job of keeping the cold at bay and the cabin warm. This time of year, I call it "The Insatiable."

It is still dark at nine o'clock when I go outside to retrieve an armload of wood. For even this short foray, I wear a parka, hat, gloves, and shoepacs. My throat and nose burn at each breath. I cover my mouth and hurry back inside.

At ten, it is light enough to see the feeder by the front porch and two boreal chickadees picking seeds. Over the last two weeks, as the temperature plummeted, the black-capped chickadees and grosbeaks that had been sharing the sunflower seeds disappeared; perhaps they moved on to the birch forests south of the Alaska Range. With their feathers puffed out for protection from the cold, the chickadees appear bigger around than they are tall. There's a fine frost around their eyes and nares, which they scrape at with their feet. It's a marvel that something so small and fragile-looking can survive in these temperatures.

At first light two days ago, I saw a red fox below the feeder, eating scattered seeds. On another day, under a tree by the woodpile, I found a frozen spruce grouse. It was intact and unmarked, as if it had frozen and toppled headlong from a limb.

I sip my tea and watch the ebon night fade and the stars wink out one by one, leaving only the gibbous moon visible in the western sky.

The horizon turns magenta, then pink, then orange, and the peaks awaken in alpenglow.

At noon I'm still at the table, drinking tea and writing letters. The sun won't rise above the mountains for another half hour, and the thermometer has not budged.

Last night I planned a short hike down to the river, thinking I might see caribou moving through the timber, or that maybe I'd cross the trail of the lynx who has been stalking the willows there. The mere thought of venturing out into such weather to look at tracks seems absurd, yet I castigate myself for being wimpy.

The mountains to the west and north have been in full sunlight for almost three hours before the light finally strikes the cabin and surrounding timber. As the sun slides west over the range, each limb, twig, and needle of the hoarfrost-draped spruce blink as if covered in crystal. Enchanted, I can no longer abide staying inside.

I will make the planned hike, but first I must prepare. I strip off my sweats and don a set of long underwear, then wool pants, wool shirt, and two pairs of socks. Next comes a sweater, down vest, and insulated shoepacs. I pull on pile overpants and my parka. I add a neck gaiter and hat. I pull down and fasten my ear flaps. Just before going out, and after nurturing the stove a last time, I put on thin polypro gloves, and over them, my heavy mittens. Outside on the porch, I yank off one mitten to feel my pockets for the waterproof matches I always carry. Before wriggling my mitten back on, I pull up my neck gaiter so that it covers my mouth and nose.

The fluffed chickadees do not stir as I walk close by their perches. The snow squeaks, almost groans, under each step. Today I will not surprise wary creatures; they will hear me long before I come close. Perhaps a moose will stand to watch as I scrunch by on the hard-packed trail. Most anything else will have long fled.

At first I am warm and worry that I am overdressed, but as I descend onto the muskeg flat below the cabin, I feel the cold seeping in, attacking my thighs, feet, and hands. My lashes frost up and stick together. I blink often to keep them from icing closed. My nostrils prickle with each breath. Already there is frost on my eyebrows, gaiter, and hat.

It takes about an hour of brisk walking to reach the river. My cabin is on a ridge little more than 300 feet higher, but it seems noticeably colder here.

The cottonwoods, spruce, and willows lining the bank wear thick coats of hoarfrost, and an ethereal, thin fog hangs over the river ice. Somewhere nearby there must be open water or overflow. In places the ice must be more than three feet thick, but I am wary and stay on the bank. Ice is always questionable where two streams converge. I grew up reading Robert Service and Jack London, and I know their stories, especially *To Build a Fire*. I've had my own brushes with thin ice, and just last week my neighbor Jeff King and his dog team broke through. It wasn't this cold then, but it was still perilous.

A dusting of snow covers my two-day-old tracks. Each night the cold draws out what little moisture there is and deposits it in fine powder. Tracking could not be better. Already I've seen skeins of vole tracks, spruce-grouse ovals, and the meandering trail of a red fox. In willows by the oxbow, I see where a moose browsed, its huge, splayed-toed tracks seared into the ice. Snowshoe-hare prints cross the trail and dapple the snow. The hare's oversized feet give support atop the powder where predators, like the fox, would only flounder. My feet, despite heavy boots, are cold, and again I marvel at these natural adaptations.

It must be very cold, for it is nearly impossible to stay warm. My neck gaiter is armored in ice, frost stings my face, and despite all the layers, I am barely comfortable, even when moving. My feet are getting numb, and I wriggle my fingers almost constantly. The sun won't reach over the bluff and onto the oxbow for another month, and the darkness makes the cold more tangible. The sun now setting on the snow-covered flanks of Mount Fellows looks warm and inviting. I cherish the illusion that Dall sheep bask in the warm, amber light there.

A raven, one of only about two dozen bird species that winters here, flaps loudly, and I stop to note its passage overhead. Downstream a short distance, the raven banks sharply over the bluff and is gone. At once I am aware of a complete, dominating silence. There's no breath of wind, movement of water, or animal sound to mar the hush—only my own breathing and the slight stirring of fabric. It is almost as if even sound has frozen.

If I remain still and control my breathing, the silence crushes in on me, becomes tangible. Thirty years ago, when I came to Alaska from Los Angeles, winter silence was the most startling contrast between the two places. On my first winter day alone in the Bush—the closest human perhaps a hundred air miles away—the utter silence, the first I'd ever experienced, unsettled me. *So this must be what deafness is like,* I recall thinking. Now I recognize that it wasn't the silence itself that unnerved me, but the underlying recognition of genuine solitude: I am alone. No one will come to my aid. Am I up to it? Can I handle it? If not, I will die here.

Years later, I still find silence to be the most remarkable, but now treasured, aspect of winter in these mountains.

Without moving, I am unable to ward off the cold. When I begin to shiver, I turn toward home. In deepening twilight, I cross the muskeg below the cabin. It is barely three o'clock, but it seems much later. A moose has crossed my trail, but I don't stop to look for it. *Nothing will stop me now,* I think. I can feel the cold gaining on me. I quicken my pace, begin to hurry. I imagine a hot cup of tea in my hands.

Cresting the last slope, I look up from the trail. I slow down and then halt.

Along the horizon, the pale blue sky fades into evening's magenta and violet pastels. A brilliant light is suspended exactly above the highest pinnacle across the river and in the park. It is so perfectly positioned that for a moment I wonder if it's an artificial light of some kind, perhaps a signal. I see, though, that it is what my father used to call "the evening star." Never have I seen such brilliance or size. For a wild, crazy moment, I think I can feel its heat, then just as swiftly reject such absurdity: What binds us this day is not heat but the cosmic cold.

Again the chill prompts me homeward, but now my steps are slower, and I keep turning toward the light until it slides behind the summit. Later, sitting in the dark in front of the stove, listening to the radio, KUAC in Fairbanks, I learn that what I saw was not a star at all, but a planet. Venus . . . at minus 50.

Tonight We Dash

Ruth Rhodes

The slack-jawed and sleepy-eyed students in my classes would never guess it, but I didn't always wear sweater sets and cameos or have so much hairspray on my head that my coiffure resembled a helmet.

They don't know that somewhere in Alaska, perhaps in the back drawer of a hotel manager's file cabinet, is a video of me, naked. I am standing in the lobby of the posh Denali Princess Hotel, surrounded by about thirty other naked people. The only person actually clothed would be the night manager, and in the video I stride toward him, lean over the front desk, and say something to him. There is no audio, because it's a security tape. For the record, I was asking for a book of matches.

I never actually saw the video, but a few days later, my boss assured me (with an unctuous grin) that I had a starring role. Apparently, the old-boy managers got together for a viewing. He expected me to be ashamed. But for nearly twenty years, long after I left Alaska and the life I'd lived there, long after those sons-of-bitches died off, one by one, my only regret is that I didn't get myself a copy. I've considered running for high political office just so it would surface.

Millions of people visit Denali National Park every summer. Most are over sixty and on package tours, usually as part of a cruise, and they step off the ship and find themselves transported by railroad deep into Alaska's interior. Young people uniformed in red and blue coats meet them at the train station, herd them onto buses, take them to their hotels, and wake them up for their 5:00 AM wildlife tour the next day. Half asleep, they take their tours, see a bear or two from the road without ever leaving the bus, and come back just in time to be herded into railcars again. They hardly know what they've seen, but they're pretty sure the brochure said it was "the real Alaska."

We—the employees—didn't exactly go out of our way to undeceive them. After all, who wants a million people running around on the tundra? Most parks are islands of wildness besieged on all sides by human development. But Denali is the reverse: over a million acres of wilderness corrupted only by a single strip of development on its eastern flank. A road with some scattered in-holdings, an airstrip, a railway station, and, at the entrance, a gaudy collection of hotels, restaurants, and tourist attractions shining like jewels in a beauty queen's plastic crown. We called this area Glitter Gulch.

I was one of the young people in a red coat carrying a clipboard and hustling people from here to there for the tour company Grayline of Alaska. At the time, I was living a double life, going to graduate school in dreary Cleveland during the school year and working summers in the park. My friends and hiking partners did all sorts of other jobs. They were bellmen and shuttle-bus drivers and hotel maids. Most of us were twentysomethings in a state of permanent transition. The work was seasonal. No one was tied down, though most of us returned summer after summer. Few longed for a "real" job or health insurance or even our own set of silverware. It was a mark of pride for me that everything I owned fit into two backpacks.

Most of the jobs in the Gulch were lousy, and mine was no exception. My boss was mean and vindictive, the company shoddy and disorganized, the hours grueling. But the primary appeal of working in the Gulch was its proximity to the backcountry, where I spent nearly every weekend of every summer. I slogged for hours through willow to get to unbelievably remote and beautiful vistas. With the help of friends, I practiced crevasse rescue and ice-axe self-arrest. I crossed the raging Toklat River, chest high, and learned about hypothermia the hard way. I met grizzly bears at close range. Wolves too.

Wild places are infused with magic, and they attract the most crazy-wonderful people. So it's ironic that of all the wild, magical places I visited in Denali, it's the Golden Spike—the Park Hotel's bar—that I recall with the most affection. When my spirit's in a pinch, when I'm feeling small, uninteresting, and bourgeois (which is rather often these days), I remember one particular night near the end of my last season.

On the night of the last full moon that summer, the usual collection of gangly employees gathered at the Spike. It was nearly midnight, and the blue-hairs were in bed. We had the bar to ourselves. In the crowd, I remember Gooch–Bell Dog–Gooch, John–Commissary–John, and Darby–Front Desk–Darby. We went by our job titles. I was Ruthe–Grayline–Ruthe.

Last call. One other bar, the Chalet, remained open three miles away, in the heart of Glitter Gulch. Now, the Denali Park Hotel had the distinction of being the only establishment actually *in* the park—it was tucked away in the woods, out of sight. The concessioner, ARAMARK, ran a shuttle bus to and from the hotel and the Gulch. They owned all the bars, anyway, and they were glad to wring money from the hands of everyone with a pulse, including employees. But I had no plans to take the bus that night.

I drank a shot of Yukon Jack and steeled myself for the task. Now or never. Last chance. Every summer before this one, I'd missed the last full moon because of school. But not this time: I'd graduated. And this was my last summer in the park. I was going to Africa as a Peace Corps volunteer, on to bigger and better adventures, I imagined. A handful of "forever seasonals" lined the bar. They'd never get the lifestyle out of their systems, but I knew I wasn't really like them.

"Tonight we dash!" I yelled over the din. A few people turned their heads. John–Bus Driver–John laughed from his barstool. He was a veteran dasher; he had done it for years. He knew what I meant.

"Tonight we dash!" I shouted at a group of female housekeepers huddled around a table. They giggled into their drinks.

"Tonight we dash!" I grinned at the bell dogs, who pounded the backs of their chairs in assent. I knew I could count on them, of all people.

I worked the room, repeating the mantra until I heard it echo back. The moment was right, the alcohol lubricating, the bar warm with the bodies of young people who had come to the edge of the wilderness because they *would* be wild.

I stood up on a table and raised my shot glass. The room stood at attention, every bottle and glass in the house lifted skyward.

"Dash! Dash! Dash!" we chanted.

I don't remember when and how our clothes started coming off. What I do know is that outside the bar, on the front deck of the hotel—the same deck where by day I marched my tourist charges to their rooms—we moonlight revelers found ourselves stripped down to nothing, save our shoes.

It was then we realized how cold Alaska really was. The chill of the night air seized our lungs with both hands and squeezed. But the cold became the motivating force—beyond our drunkenness, beyond our obligations to the tradition of The Dash. The only course left to us was to run. Our destination: the Chalet Bar. Get there before close.

The road from the Park Hotel to Highway 1 and Glitter Gulch was wide, dark, and deserted, and we moved like a heard of caribou, respectfully spaced and protective of each other. We soon warmed up enough to feel our extremities, which shook, jiggled, and dangled in the cold air in a way that's surprising unless you've actually run naked before. The moonlight poured down on the empty road and blanketed the trees around us. Sugarloaf Mountain sparkled in a backdrop of stars. It was breathtaking. Simultaneously vulnerable and invincible, we ran. The sound of our shoes pounding the pavement echoed off the canyon.

When we reached the highway, bright lights lit us up like the white-bellied Alaska rats we were. Traffic slowed to a crawl as it passed us. Some people stopped and got out of their cars. We joked that this must be what life was like for the bears on the wildlife tour.

At the Nenana River Bridge, we stopped for stragglers. That was when someone spotted the bonfire over at Era Helicopters.

Era's pilots kept to themselves. They were middle-aged Vietnam vets who had flown choppers in the war and now made their living taking wealthy tourists on sightseeing trips. It occurred to me, as we approached their camp, that they might consider us a hostile force. We did startle them, gluing them to their folding chairs for a time. But after the initial shock wore off, they stood up and welcomed us rather warmly. So warmly, in fact, that when I considered it later, it was if they had been sitting around, staring at their fire, wondering when a group of naked young people was going to come rushing out of the dark to dance around their campfire.

Flushed and alive in the light and heat of the flames, we circled and circled in a spontaneous dance of our own design, and for the first time, we revelers really looked at one another. Most of the alcohol had evaporated from our systems, and yet we weren't really sober. We were traveling through a wilderness of our own making. Suddenly, like a flock of birds, we turned and faded back into the dark, back to the road and toward our destination, leaving the pilots to resume their seats and contemplate the events of the night.

We made one last stop before the Chalet—the Denali Princess Hotel. Now, none of the runners were Princess employees. *Those* people didn't mix. But that didn't stop us from entering their brightly lit lobby and greeting their guests. In fact, a stop at Princess was part of the Dash ritual, as was the obligatory request for matches.

A few minutes after leaving the Princess Hotel, we made it to the Chalet Bar. I'm vague on the details again here, but when we emerged, we found that Bryan–Bus Driver–Bryan had commandeered a shuttle for us. By "commandeered" I mean that he stole it—technically, his shift was over, and his bus should have gone to the garage. But he'd followed us from the Spike—after loyally gathering up all our clothes from the hotel deck and tossing them into the back of the bus. He then boldly parked in front of the Chalet and kept the engine running. At least someone was thinking ahead.

We shrieked with glee and appreciation for the bus, and for our clothes. But we didn't put them on immediately. We rode home naked—singing and shouting like a group of elementary school kids coming home from a field trip—and halfway there, we started to chant: "Bus driver naked! Bus driver naked!" Bryan pulled over and accepted the challenge like a good sport.

Bryan–Bus Driver–Bryan wrote to me—many letters—while I was in Peace Corps, but it's been ages since I've heard from him. I don't have a current address. When I sent him a Christmas card last year, complete with pictures of husband, kid, dog, and cat, I addressed it to "Bus Garage, Denali Park," but the idea was silly, because the park is closed for the winter, and who knows if he still works there. They've long since demolished the Denali Park Hotel, the Golden Spike along with it.

I mailed it, and it never came back, but that doesn't mean anything. It couldn't have reached its destination, since I really meant to send it back through time. If I could only do that, I wouldn't even need to write to Bryan. I'd just write to my twentysomething self. I guess that's who I really want to get in touch with anyway. If I could do that, I'd send her Post-it notes with little pieces of advice on them. "Don't speed while passing through Provo, Utah." "Floss regularly." And "If he seems like a total stoner, he probably is."

Maybe she'd crumple them up and toss them away. After all, why would she heed the advice of a tired, middle-aged, overworked mother who doesn't even drink wine anymore because it gives her headaches?

But then again, maybe she'd be kind enough to drop me a line. To give me a bit of advice of her own. And I think I know what she'd say. Using the shorthand of our accumulated wisdom, she'd write these words, and they would ring true across the years: "Tonight we dash."

A Chance Encounter

Robert Cornelius

I drove my patrol car lazily along the South Rim Drive in Black Canyon of the Gunnison National Park and pulled into the parking area at the end of the road, a place called High Point, which serves as the trailhead for the Warner Nature Trail. I grabbed my canteen and a small pack holding a first-aid kit and a pair of binoculars.

I was three months away from ending my thirty-three-year career as a park ranger. It was a warm, sunny Colorado spring morning as I began my walk down the trail toward Warner Point, a mile away. The fragrance of pine and sage scented the air. The Warner Trail serpentines up and down, and from one side to the other, along a narrow ridge. To the south lies the Uncompahgre Valley, and on the horizon is the broken, jagged, snowcapped profile of the San Juan Mountains and the Uncompahgre Plateau. To the north, the dark cliffs of the Black Canyon were bathed in the morning light. As I walked along, I thought of how the rocky ridge had protected the piñons and junipers from centuries of fire. Some of the gnarled trees shading me had been anchored among the rocks for more than six hundred years.

The jingle of the keys on my duty belt and the occasional crackle of the park radio reminded me of the paperwork blizzard that would await me when I returned to my office at the other end of the road. I decided to put that out of my mind and to enjoy these few quiet moments. After all, this was ranger work too.

I continued along the trail, stopping to briefly chat with morning hikers who were heading back toward the parking area. They clutched trail brochures but were still full of questions:

"Are those sand dunes below?"

"How deep is the canyon?"

"Why do you wear a gun?"

"Is that a mountain lion track I saw in the dried mud?"

"How far is it to the next gas station?"

I enjoyed most of the questions and remained patient with those I'd answered a thousand times before.

As I started up the last hill, before the end of the trail and Warner Point, I encountered a father and his young son. The boy, who looked to be about ten, bubbled with energy and was anxious to get to the end of the trail. But the mountain air was taking its toll on his father, who kept encouraging the boy to slow down, even as he kept bouncing on ahead. I fell in behind the two, and soon all three of us were at the end of the trail.

The father and son looked at the scene before them. The view is dramatic: mountains, plateaus, forests, with the highlight being the canyon. The Painted Wall—a 2,300-foot cliff—is prominent. The Gunnison River can be seen and heard as it falls rapidly in its wild pursuit of a spot to rest.

I answered several questions from the father. Then questions about the river, the canyon, and the local animals flooded from the boy's mouth. His father decided he needed to come to my rescue. He told his son that the ranger probably had important things to do in the area. He told his son that he'd managed to pick my brain clean.

After answering one last question, I excused myself and walked the short distance to the head of a near vertical ravine at the far side of the viewing area. I casually surveyed the area along the rim, and to my surprise, less than 50 feet away stood a large Rocky Mountain bighorn sheep. He was a beautiful specimen with the classic three-quarter curl. He paid me little mind and continued to move gracefully among the rocks and brush, foraging for tasty spring foliage.

I walked back to find the father still trying to catch his breath and the son now fidgeting in the dirt. Having been in one place for what he thought was long enough, the boy was begging his dad to get going back down the trail.

I interrupted the boy's pleading. "Would you like to see something neat?"

"What?" he asked.

"You'll see." The boy and his father followed me to the top of the nearby ravine. When we arrived, I pointed to the ram and said, "Look over there!"

The boy looked and looked but saw nothing. As God intended, the bighorn blended in perfectly with the natural background. But after a great deal of pointing by me and then his father, the boy said, "Oh . . . *wow!*"

The three of us lingered, marveling at the beauty and the majesty of the ram.

When the father decided it was finally time to head back to the car, the boy, who ten minutes before had been so anxious to leave, now wanted to stay. He reluctantly complied, and as they headed out, the boy looked back again and again, trying to get one last glimpse of the spectacular animal. I followed a short distance behind the pair, and a ways down the trail, I heard the boy say, "I'll never forget this for the rest of my life!"

Having heard his excited words, I thought, *That's what the national parks are all about.* I wondered if I had made a difference in his life, the way a park naturalist had made in mine so long ago. When I was nine years old, my dad and I joined a nature hike near El Capitan in Yosemite. Leading the hike was a park naturalist who introduced me to the meadows, forest, waterfalls, and wildlife, and I marveled at them. It was that guided hike that sparked a desire within me to someday work for the National Park Service.

Soon my Park Service career would be coming to an end. But I like to think I passed the torch that day, through a chance encounter that I arranged between a young boy and a bighorn sheep.

Contributors

Elizabeth Arnold spent about a year as a wrangler on a guest ranch in Jackson Hole, Wyoming. During that time, she guided trail rides, cooked on backcountry pack-trips, and wrangled in a wilderness hunting camp. She earned her MA in English from Arcadia University in Philadelphia, Pennsylvania. She is presently pursuing an MFA from the Rainier Writing Workshop in Tacoma, Washington. Her work has appeared in the *Minnemingo Review* and *The Fridge Door*. Elizabeth currently lives on a small farm in Central Pennsylvania, where she enjoys hiking and riding and training her horses. She is at work on a full-length collection of essays based on her time in Wyoming.

For her master's degree in wildlife biology, **Mary Beth Baptiste** researched human-bear interaction at Shenandoah National Park. She later worked at Cumberland Gap and Grand Teton National Parks. After seven years at Grand Teton, she moved to Laramie, Wyoming, where she now lives with her husband, Richard. Her employment history, while suspect, provides fertile ground for writing material: soda jerk, fire-tower lookout, lab technician, land steward, school counselor, substance-abuse counselor, yoga teacher, wildlife biologist, technical writer, bookstore clerk, environmental scientist, and nonprofit development director. When she's not writing, Mary Beth enjoys hiking, cross-country skiing, dancing, and spending time with friends, especially when chocolate is involved. She was a 2009 resident at the Jentel Artist Residency Program in Banner, Wyoming, and has won several writing awards, including the Doubleday Award for Creative Writing. Her work has appeared in *Vermont Literary Review, Copper Nickel, Newsweek, Wyoming Wildlife, Stonehill Alumni Magazine,* and two other anthologies.

Matthew Bowser is a former trail dog living in the extreme northwest corner of Montana. He recently traded in his shovel for a pen and is now the Forest Watch Coordinator for a tiny grassroots organization focused on permanently protecting the last remaining roadless cores of a rare and critical valley. The knowledge he discovered while digging into Yellowstone opened the door and propelled him into a much larger world than he had known before: the heart of the volcano.

In 1995, **Christine Byl** took her first job on a trail crew in Glacier National Park, where she worked until 2002. Since then she has worked on trail crews for the U.S. Forest Service in Cordova, Alaska, and Denali National Park. Her home base is a yurt located on a few acres of tundra just north of Denali in Healy, Alaska, where she lives with her husband and two sled dogs. She and her husband now run a small contracting business focused on designing and building trails, primarily on public lands. The essay in this collection was excerpted from *Dirt Work: An Education on the Ground,* her nonfiction manuscript in progress about trail work, tools, and wilderness. Other essays have been published in the anthologies *A Mile in Her Boots: Women Who Work in the Wild* and *Cold Flashes: Snapshots of Alaska.* Her fiction has appeared in *Glimmer Train, Bellingham Review, Lumberyard, Crazyhorse,* and other journals. When not reading, writing, or working on trails, Christine digs mountain adventures, building projects, and anything that happens in the snow.

Robert Cornelius was born and raised in the Bay Area and graduated from the University of California, Berkeley, in 1969 with a degree in geography. He began his career with the National Park Service first as a wide-eyed ranger at Grand Canyon National Park. After his initial assignment on the South Rim, he moved to the inner canyon and was stationed with his horse at Phantom Ranch. In 1973, he transferred to Dinosaur National Monument, where he served as the park's river ranger, boating extensively on the Green and Yampa Rivers. He later transferred to Glen Canyon National Recreation Area, Rainbow Bridge National Monument, Curecanti National Recreation Area, and Black Canyon of the Gunnison National Park, where he and his wife raised two daughters, and where he spent the final twenty-five years of his thirty-three-year career. After retiring from the Park Service in 2002, he began working for the Montrose Police Department at the Montrose Animal Shelter, where he enjoys his second passion: dogs. Bob once loathed folks in motor homes, but now finds himself looking forward to touring all the parks at which he didn't work while driving his own. He began writing about his park adventures soon after he retired, and he guarantees his high school English teacher would turn over in her grave if she knew he'd authored published works.

Troy Davis has worked seasonally as a biologist for the Bureau of Land Management, the U.S. Fish and Wildlife Service, and the National Park Service. He has been lucky enough to conduct fieldwork in places as beautiful as the beaches of Florida, the Cascade Range of Oregon, and the rainforests of Central America. His work has allowed him to observe and learn about sharks, spotted owls, kangaroo rats, sea turtles, plovers, terns, beach mice, elk, grizzlies, bison, raccoons, cougars, and dolphins. His experiences with these and other creatures (especially cats, for which he holds a special fondness) has impressed on him that the truest expression of humility is to be found in one's own personal ratio of "seeking" to "finding." Whether it was for jaguar or pronghorn, he has typically done much searching and precious little seeing. In retrospect, he would not have it any other way.

Monica Delmartini has worked in Sequoia and Kings Canyon National Parks for seven years. She spends half the year prowling the woods as a fire-effects monitor and the other half baking beautiful loaves of bread.

Keith Ekiss is a Jones Lecturer in Creative Writing at Stanford University and a former Wallace Stegner Fellow in poetry. He is the past recipient of scholarships and residencies from the Bread Loaf and Squaw Valley Writers' Conferences, Santa Fe Art Institute, and the Petrified Forest National Park. His poems— and his translations of the Costa Rican poet Eunice Odio—have appeared in *Gulf Coast, Harvard Review, New England Review, Modern Poetry in Translation, The Christian Science Monitor,* and elsewhere. *Pima Road Notebook,* his first book, was published by New Issues Poetry and Prose in 2010.

Mary Emerick has lived and worked in nine national parks. She has been a wildland firefighter, a cave tour guide, a tree planter, a wilderness ranger, and a naturalist. Her writing has appeared in several anthologies and magazines. She currently lives in a log cabin in the Wallowa Mountains of Northeast Oregon, where she works for the U.S. Forest Service as a wilderness, trails, and recreation manager. Her blog can be found at www. mountainsskin.blogspot.com.

Joseph Flannery lived and worked seasonally in Yellowstone National Park for three years. He now lives in Tahoe City, California, and enjoys skiing, backpacking, and mountain biking with his girlfriend and puppy. Joseph is currently writing a collection of essays on his time spent in Yellowstone.

Melanie Dylan Fox is a nature writer and educator who has lived throughout the United States and Europe, and who spent many seasons working in California's Sequoia National Park. In addition to receiving a notable mention in *Best American Essays* and an AWP Intro Award, her work has appeared in literary journals such as *Bayou Magazine*, *Fourth Genre*, and *Flyway*, and also in the anthologies *American Nature Writing* and *Figuring Animals: Essays on Animal Images in Art, Literature, Philosophy, & Popular Culture*. She has work forthcoming in the collection *Between Song and Story: Essays for the Twenty-First Century*, to be published by Autumn House Press. Her writing focuses on the intricacies of place, and she is particularly interested in the portrayal of animals in science, folklore, and myth in order to meditate on the complexities of human-animal relationships. She teaches literature and writing courses in nature and environmental writing in Chatham University's low-residency MFA program, teaches English at Radford University, and works as a senior technical editor with Bennett Aerospace. She currently makes her home at the confluence of the Blue Ridge and Appalachian Mountains, in the New River Valley of southwestern Virginia.

An associate professor at Elon University, **Cassandra Kircher** is the recipient of Iowa State University's 2009 Notes from the Field Contest. Her essays have been published in *Front Range Review*, *Red Mountain Review*, *Flyway*, and *Interdisciplinary Studies for Literature and the Environment*. She is completing a manuscript that is focused on her seven years working for the National Park Service.

Jeremy Pataky earned an MFA in poetry from the University of Montana and a Certificate in Nonprofit Management from The Foraker Group and University of Alaska, Fairbanks. His work has appeared in *Black Warrior Review, Cirque, Northern Review, The Southeast Review, Anchorage Daily News,* and many other publications, and has been featured on Alaska Public Radio. His chapbook, *Fata Morgana,* was released digitally by Blue Hour Press. He has worked as a wilderness guide, freelance writer, and university instructor, and he is the executive director of the Wrangell Mountains Center. He started the Still North Reading and Performance Series in south-central Alaska and is a founding director of 49 Alaska Writing Center.

Ruth Rhodes's love of wild and remote places began when she was twenty-five and took a summer job with a tour company in Denali National Park. After three seasons in Alaska and a two-year stint in the Peace Corps, she worked for nearly a decade in national parks in the Northwest, both as a ranger and as an environmental educator. She now lives a comparatively tame life in California, teaching English at College of the Redwoods and raising two boys with the help of her husband. Every day, however, she contemplates escape, in some way or another. "When they make a diaper bag big enough for four sleeping bags," she says, "we're outta here."

Nathan Rice was born and bred in the Pacific Northwest and has lived, worked, and roamed around the Western Hemisphere. The Cascades are deep in his bones.

Almost twenty-five years have passed since the events in **Christa Sadler**'s essay "No Turning Back," yet her memories of it are as clear as yesterday.

Sometimes I find it hard to believe I'm still here, but then I think I don't have much choice in the matter. A lot has changed since those early days. In addition to the Grand Canyon, I now work in the extraordinary wilderness of Alaska and the Yukon. I watch glaciers calving, and float near bears and icebergs. I build homes in Nicaragua every winter and work on the border between Arizona and Mexico, trying to help ease the struggles of people crossing to find a better life in the United States. I write books and articles about dinosaurs and other charismatic creatures of the ancient world, and I've got a couple in the hopper. I work with young kids in the outdoors, studying the land, fossils, writing, and the art of joy. I write, teach, cry, and laugh in the wide-open spaces of our continent, and give thanks every day for those places. And I realize that boatmen are not mythical heroes, as I once thought, but I am prouder to belong to this group than of any other thing in my life. Whitewater still makes my heart quicken, but I now recognize landmarks in the rapids. I usually hang onto my oars, and have learned how to control my boat—most of the time. I can relax enough now to think of natural history and stories, poetry and art, and to talk with people about them as we drift downstream. But the Colorado River and her Grand Canyon still inspire me, still teach and humble me. I watch the guests on our trips go through the same cycle I experienced, from anxiety and fear to acceptance and wonder. I realize that a journey is born with each new trip, and I'm honored to be part of it.

Nicole Sheets recently moved to Spokane from Salt Lake City, where she completed a PhD in literature and creative writing from the University of Utah and developed an appetite for desert light and scenic rocks. Her work has appeared in *Western*

Humanities Review, Quarterly West, North Dakota Quarterly, Geez Magazine, Jesus Girls: True Tales of Growing Up Female and Evangelical, and in a number of newspapers and magazines in her home state of West Virginia. She has essays forthcoming in *Mid-American Review* (as an AWP Intro Award winner), *Cream City Review, Sonora Review, Western Humanities Review,* and *Tampa Review.* Nicole taught English as a Peace Corps volunteer in Moldova, and for the last six summers, she's been on the faculty of the West Virginia Governor's Honors Academy, where she's offered cooking and creative writing classes to high school students. She is now writing a collection of essays about growing up in an evangelical church and a blog (ThrippieGalore!) about thrift shopping, our complex relationships with our stuff, and adjusting to life in the Pacific Northwest. Nicole is a visiting assistant professor in the English department at Whitworth University.

Seth Slater received his MFA from Antioch University, Los Angeles. He is a former newspaper reporter and editor who writes poetry, short stories, and essays. "An Admirable Hard Start" describes events that took place during a season he spent working as a wrangler and trail guide for a pack outfit in the Eastern Sierra. Slater has, at various times, worked as a deckhand aboard a commercial fishing boat in Alaska, a volunteer for the California State Parks system, a scuba instructor in Southern California, and a civilian dolphin trainer for the U.S. Navy. He was a night-shift taxi driver on Alaska's Kenai Peninsula and has twice camped his way across the southern states in a pickup truck, accompanied by a Siberian husky and a kayak. He was an invited reader at the West Hollywood Book Fair in 2009, and his short story "The Job" was anthologized by DimeStories Live Showcase on the CD *Five & Dime* in 2008. He currently lives with his wife, Erin, in San Diego, where he teaches creative writing for the University of California and is at work on his first novel.

Janet Smith began college at thirty-five after a string of jobs in Yosemite National Park. She graduated with an MFA in creative nonfiction from the University of Minnesota in 2001. She is a past recipient of a Nevada Arts Board Fellowship in poetry and has been nominated for a Pushcart Prize. Her first book of poetry, *All of a Sudden Nothing Happened,* was published in 2010. She is on faculty in the English department at Lake Tahoe Community College.

A forty-five-year resident of Alaska, **Tom Walker** lives in a log house on the boundary of Denali National Park. The award-winning author of fourteen books on Alaska's natural history (including collections of wildlife photography), he is an ardent student of the natural world. He has been a wilderness guide, a log-home builder, and a conservation officer, and has been self-employed as a freelance writer and photographer since 1971. His two-volume history of Denali Park's early years took thirty years to complete.

Join the community. Share your park stories.
www.pvstories.net

www.bonafidebooks.com